It's All Elementary

It's All Elementary

From Atoms to the Quantum World of Quarks, Leptons, and Gluons

By Necia H. Apfel

LOTHROP, LEE & SHEPARD BOOKS / NEW YORK

To my husband, Don

Library of Congress Cataloging in Publication Data

Apfel, Necia H. / It's all elementary. / Summary: Traces the search leading to the discovery of the smallest bits of matter, pieces too small to be subdivided, and discusses recent developments in the field of particle physics, or study of the invisible microworld of elementary particles. 1. Particles (Nuclear physics)—Juvenile literature. [1. Particles (Nuclear physics) 2. Nuclear physics. 3. Physics] I. Title. QC793.27.A63 1985
539.7'21   84-9718 ISBN 0-688-04092-6 (pbk.)   ISBN 0-688-04093-4 (lib. bdg.)

Contents

Preface

FIFTY YEARS AGO the public was beginning to read about a new theory in physics called "relativity." It presented new and strange concepts, many of which were unbelievable and, at first, unacceptable to the average person. Today, although not many people truly understand what this important theory is all about, most have heard of it and probably, without realizing it, benefit from it every day. Its simpler concepts are now taught in many high school physics courses and college students, especially those who are majoring in science, go further into it. Albert Einstein's face is now a familiar one and he is recognized internationally as having been one of the greatest scientists who ever lived.

Today, the "quantum theory," which is as important and as revolutionary as relativity, is now making its way into the public consciousness. Although its construction began before Einstein's theory, only recently has it caught the attention of the popular press. Now most of us have heard about infinitesimally small particles called "quarks" and "gluons." Many of us have also heard about enormous circular machines that hurl subatomic bits of matter at each other in incredible velocities to reveal the secrets of the universe around us.

As I write these words, it has just been reported that the 1984 Nobel Prize in Physics has been awarded to Carl Rubbia of Italy and Simon van der Meer of the Netherlands for their "decisive contributions to the large project that led to the discovery of the field particles W and Z, communicators of the weak interaction." The detection of these particular particles is part of a long search for the ultimate building blocks of the universe. Unlike Einstein's relativity theory, that search and the theories that have encouraged it have been the work of hundreds of scientists. That search is the subject of this book.

Because these ideas are the basis for much of our scientific research today, it is essential that we be exposed to them as early in our education as possible. We must become familiar with them and incorporate them into our thinking, becoming as conversant with the realm of inner space—the subatomic, subnuclear world of quarks, leptons, and gluons—as we are with areas of outer space—the planets, stars, and galaxies. This book is for future scientists as well as for the adult who may not be a scientist but wants to learn what "particle physics" is all about.

Since the readers to whom this book is addressed may not have had training in advanced physics and mathematics, the discussion here cannot be as precise or complete as it would be if mathematical equations and the language of advanced physics were used. My purpose, however, is not to write a definitive text but rather to present an overall view, an introduction to a very complex and difficult subject.

I wish to express my appreciation and thanks to Dr. Jonathan Schonfeld of the Fermi National Laboratory who read the manuscript several times and spent many hours discussing it with me. His suggestions and criticisms were invaluable. I also thank Dr. Gerald Feinberg of Columbia University for reviewing the manuscript and offering numerous ideas for its improvement.

Lastly, I thank my husband, Don, for his patience and love during all the months of writing and rewriting this book, even if, too often, it meant that dinner was neither ready nor even planned.
                                                        Necia H. Apfel
                                                        November, 1984

1

The Search Begins

WHAT ARE THE THINGS around you made of? Some are solid objects like this book or the chair on which you are sitting. Others, such as water and fruit juices, are liquid. And of course, the air you are breathing is a gas. But all of it is "matter." Everything you can see or feel is matter. In fact, you are made of matter.

There are so many kinds of matter that to list them all here would not be possible. Each has its own particular characteristics, or "properties," that make it different from any other. For example, molasses flows very slowly out of a bottle while milk spills out rapidly. Scientists say that molasses has a greater "viscosity" than milk. Viscosity is one property of matter.

Another property is "density," which is a measure of how much matter a particular substance has in a given volume of space. A Ping-Pong ball weighs less than a lead ball of the same size because lead has a greater density than the air within the Ping-Pong ball or the plastic that it is made of; there is, therefore, more matter in the lead ball. It has what scientists call greater "mass." The lead ball, for example, will sink in a bucket of water because lead is denser than water, but the Ping-Pong ball will float because air is less dense.

Other properties of matter are the temperatures at which it melts, boils, or freezes; its hardness; and whether or not it will conduct electricity or can be magnetized. There are also chemical properties that determine how a substance reacts with other materials to produce other kinds of matter. A familiar example of this occurs when iron combines with oxygen to form "iron oxide," or rust. Iron and oxygen are two kinds of matter, each with its own unique properties. Iron oxide is a third kind of matter, quite different from the other two.

Iron and oxygen are very special kinds of matter, however, which scientists call "elements." An element can be combined with other elements but it cannot be broken down into simpler substances. Other elements include gold, silver, lithium, aluminum, and carbon. There are about ninety natural elements existing here on earth. In laboratories, scientists have produced many artificial ones as well so that there are over one hundred known elements. The artificial elements are believed to have been present on earth millions or billions of years ago, but they disintegrated long ago into other elements. There are some natural elements, called "radioactive" elements, that are currently disintegrating in the same manner, only more slowly. In a few billion years, they also will only exist on earth in laboratories.

When elements combine with each other, they form "compounds." Rust is a compound. So are water, salt, and glass. Your fingernail is a compound as is the paper in this book. In fact, most kinds of matter are compounds. To become a particular compound, the elements in the material must be in definite proportions and arranged in a specific manner. For example, to make water you must have two parts of hydrogen to one part of oxygen. In chemistry this is written "H_2O." Table salt, another compound, is composed of equal parts of the element sodium (Na) and the element chlorine (Cl). Its chemical symbol therefore is "NaCl." Each of the more than one hundred elements has its own symbol or abbreviation. You will find them all listed in Table 1 on pages 18–19.

The properties of a compound depend upon the elements of which it is made. But what makes the elements differ from each other? This question was raised thousands of years ago and started philosophers and scientists on a search that led to more questions: What is matter? What is it made out of? How small a bit of matter can there be? The search has been long and, at times, difficult. In recent centuries it has involved many fields of science, including chemistry, physics, and astronomy. This book will explore the contributions made by all of these scientific areas, and the questions that are currently being asked by researchers.

Once it was discovered that the elements could not be decomposed into simpler substances, scientists wondered: What is the smallest bit of elemental material possible? How tiny a piece of iron or carbon, for example, could there be? Such a speck of matter, if it could not be broken up further, would be an "elementary particle," a basic or fundamental building block of the universe. This is what researchers set out to find.

Today the name for these studies is "particle physics," and an elementary particle is described as being not only indivisible and without internal structure, but also dimensionless. It does not occupy any space and is therefore considered "pointlike," without any volume. Looking for such a particle has led scientists into a very strange and hard-to-believe domain that lies at the submicroscopic level. This micro-world cannot be understood by relying solely upon the world we experience through our unaided senses. It cannot easily be illustrated in drawings or in photographs; it cannot be visualized and does not agree with our common sense. Scientists can understand and describe it in exact terms using mathematical instruments. But even they often have difficulty expressing its concepts in words that we all can understand.

Part of this difficulty arises from the fact that we try to describe this unseen and unfelt world with words that were originally intended for our everyday world—the macroworld that we can see and feel. It is somewhat like Christopher Columbus trying to describe the workings of a television set or a computer, neither of which he could ever have imagined.

The search for elementary particles began with the ancient Greeks, who originated many of the ideas about them. However, the Greeks were not scientists, for although they had many ideas about the world, they didn't try to prove them with experiments. They just thought about these ideas and simply decided which were right and which were wrong. Many times they were wrong, but they had no way of knowing of their errors because they did not try to test any of their ideas.

Today, to explain some phenomenon or experimental result, a scientist first proposes a "hypothesis." In fact, several hypotheses may be advanced, but they all must agree with previous observations or experiments and must be able to be tested by further observations or experiments.

If one or more hypotheses appear to be correct and they fit together without contradicting each other, they are grouped together to form a "theory." At some future time, however, a theory may be challenged by new hypotheses and subjected to further testing. The more a theory is tested and found to be correct, the more scientifically accepted it becomes as a model that accurately describes the behavior of nature. There is, however, always the possibility that some new evidence will require it to be revised or even replaced.

No one can guarantee that any theory is the absolute truth.

The ancient Greeks did not understand this concept of science. They believed that if they pondered some phenomenon long enough, they could discover the truth about it. If they arrived at what they believed was a logical answer, they considered it correct. One such conclusion was that everything in the world was made up of combinations of only four basic substances—earth, air, water, and fire. These substances were called "elements." Everything else was believed to be a combination of these four elements. Today we know that the ancient Greek concept about elements was incorrect, but scientists still use the same word "element" to describe basic substances.

The idea of elementary particles was first introduced by the Greek philosopher Democritus in about 450 B.C. He suggested that everything was composed of very small bits of matter that could not be divided any further. He called these bits of matter "atoms," which means "indivisible" in Greek. He believed that there were many different kinds of atoms and that all substances were simply different combinations of these atoms.

Fermilab.

The Greek philosopher Democritus, who first introduced the idea of elementary particles.

Democritus had no more proof of his ideas than did the Greeks who believed in the four-element concept. He didn't know what an atom was or how big it might be, nor did he perform any experiments to find out. There were many learned people of his day, and even centuries later, who rejected such an idea as absurd. Today we are amazed at how close to the truth he came.

However, to pursue any type of scientific investigation requires experimentation. The Greeks didn't perform experiments and unfortunately there was very little interest in doing them up through medieval times. The only people who did any testing of various substances during the Middle Ages were called "alchemists." In their small laboratories they heated, burned, melted, evaporated, and tried all possible

A reconstruction of an alchemist's laboratory.
History of Astronomy Collection, Price Photographic Archive, Adler Planetarium.

combinations of any materials they could obtain. Their interest in performing these tests was for quite unscientific reasons, but in the process they did manage to identify many elements and compounds. What they really were searching for was a method of turning base metals, such as lead and copper, into the precious metals, gold and silver. Fame and fortune would surely have been given to anyone who had succeeded in making such an alteration. But alas, none did.

In their numerous attempts at such an impossible task, many alchemists became frauds and resorted to trickery and quackery to earn their fortunes. The profession eventually gained a very bad reputation. No honest experimenter wanted to be called an alchemist. By the seventeenth century, the word "alchemist" had been changed to "chemist." And the science of chemistry made a fresh start.

Chemistry was not the only science that gained new stimulation at this time. It was a period of great scientific achievement in all fields. Optics, sound, electricity, and magnetism were some of the many areas that were explored. As we shall see, discoveries in these fields eventually helped scientists in their search for the nature of matter.

However, it was the chemists who, by their many experiments, established the foundations for the modern theory of the atom. Their investigations were done not in an attempt to produce gold or silver, but to find out more about the world around them. The questions that they asked themselves were: Which substances are truly basic elements? Which are compounds? What are the properties of these elements and compounds? How do they differ from other elements or compounds?

By the middle of the seventeenth century many elements had been identified, including mercury, sulfur, and lead, and the English chemist Robert Boyle was able to scientifically define the term. An element, he said, is a basic substance that can be combined with other elements to form compounds, but it cannot be broken down into any simpler substance once it is separated out of a compound. This definition is still used today.

But why did elements differ from each other? Why did each have its own unique properties? Some were metallic in their normal state, while others were gaseous. Some combined easily with other elements; others did not. Some were better conductors of electricity; others proved to be excellent insulators. These and other properties identified each chemical element. No one knew why these properties existed.

In 1808 John Dalton, another English chemist, helped to revive Democritus's ancient ideas about atoms. Dalton suggested that the elements differed from each other because each one was made up of a specific kind of atom. For example, a chunk of pure lead contained only atoms of lead, and a cloud of hydrogen gas had only hydrogen atoms in it. The atoms of each element differed from each other, Dalton said, by their sizes and weights. He had no way of knowing how much an atom weighed or how big it was, but this introduction of the concept of "atomic weights" led to many further experiments and discoveries.

Nineteenth-century chemists who followed Dalton soon found ways of obtaining at least the relative weights of atoms. Because they couldn't isolate an individual atom, they instead measured the quantity and weight of each element that was separated out of a specific compound, such as copper oxide or hydrogen chloride. They then made deductions about the elements' chemical behavior, and from that calculated the relative weight of each element and therefore of each kind of atom. In this way they determined that the lightest atom is a hydrogen atom.

These early chemists didn't know how very tiny such an atom might be. A toy balloon filled with hydrogen atoms would hold some one hundred million million billion (10^{23}) of them. Here on earth hydrogen, such as that in the balloon, is a gas although it is often found combined with other elements to make liquid or solid substances. For example, two hydrogen atoms combined with one oxygen atom make a "molecule" of ordinary water. A molecule is the smallest portion of a substance that can exist independently and still retain the chemical properties of the original substance. If a molecule is broken down into the atoms it is made up of, it no longer has its original properties.

During the nineteenth century, as more experiments were conducted, the list of known elements, along with their relative weights and their other properties, continued to grow. Dozens were recognized by 1850, but the collection appeared to have no order. However, as happens in any field of science, chemists sought to classify and arrange this disorganized array of information.

In 1869, after many attempts by others, the Russian chemist Dmitri Ivanovich Mendeleev brought order to the hodgepodge collection. He first listed all the elements according to their atomic weights. As he went down the list, he noted that the same kinds of chemical behavior, or properties, tended to repeat themselves with regularity, or periodically. For example, lithium is a metal that can be made to produce a strong alkali (a substance used, sometimes in medications, to neutralize acids). Eight elements further down Mendeleev's list of elements is sodium, which also has this property. And eight beyond sodium is potassium, another alkali-producing metal. Mendeleev found other groups of elements whose chemical behavior was also very much alike. He took his list and arranged the elements into columns according to these

Table 1. THE PERIODIC TABLE OF THE ELEMENTS

The number in the lower right-hand corner of each box is that element's atomic weight. Its symbol is in the left-hand corner. Above its name is its atomic number.

1 Hydrogen (H) 1.008								
3 Lithium (Li) 6.939	4 Beryllium (Be) 9.012							
11 Sodium (Na) 22.99	12 Magnesium (Mg) 24.312							
19 Potassium (K) 39.102	20 Calcium (Ca) 40.08	21 Scandium (Sc) 44.956	22 Titanium (Ti) 47.90	23 Vanadium (V) 50.942	24 Chromium (Cr) 51.996	25 Manganese (Mn) 54.938	26 Iron (Fe) 55.847	27 Coba (Co) 58
37 Rubidium (Rb) 85.47	38 Strontium (Sr) 87.62	39 Yttrium (Y) 88.905	40 Zirconium (Zr) 91.22	41 Niobium (Nb) 92.906	42 Molydenum (Mo) 95.94	43 Technetium (Tc) 98.91	44 Ruthenium (Ru) 101.07	45 Rhodi (Rh) 10
55 Cesium (Cs) 132.905	56 Barium (Ba) 137.34	57 Lanthanum (La) 138.91	58 Cerium (Ce) 140.12	59 Praseodymium (Pr) 140.907	60 Neodymium (Nd) 144.24	61 Promethium (Pm) 145.	62 Samarium (Sm) 150.35	63 Europi (Eu) 1
			72 Hafnium (Hf) 178.49	73 Tantalum (Ta) 180.948	74 Tungsten (W) 183.85	75 Rhenium (Re) 186.2	76 Osmium (Os) 190.2	77 Iridiu (Ir) 1
87 Francium (Fr) 223.	88 Radium (Ra) 226.05	89 Actinium (Ac) 227.	90 Thorium (Th) 232.038	91 Protactinium (Pa) 231.	92 Uranium (U) 238.03	93 Neptunium (Np) 237.	94 Plutonium (Pu) 242.	95 Americ (Am)
			104 Rutherfordium (Rf) 261.	105 Hahnium (Ha) 262.				

								2 Helium (He) 4.003
			5 Boron (B) 10.811	6 Carbon (C) 12.011	7 Nitrogen (N) 14,007	8 Oxygen (O) 15.999	9 Fluorine (F) 18.998	10 Neon (Ne) 20.183
			13 Aluminum (Al) 26.982	14 Silicon (Si) 28.086	15 Phosphorus (P) 30.974	16 Sulfur (S) 32.064	17 Chlorine (Cl) 35.453	18 Argon (Ar) 39.948
28 Nickel i) 58.71	29 Copper (Cu) 63.54	30 Zinc (Zn) 65.37	31 Gallium (Ga) 69.72	32 Germanium (Ge) 72.59	33 Arsenic (As) 74.922	34 Selenium (Se) 78.96	35 Bromine (Br) 79.909	36 Krypton (Kr) 83.80
46 alladium d) 106.4	47 Silver (Ag) 107.87	48 Cadmium (Cd) 112.40	49 Indium (In) 114.82	50 Tin (Sn) 118.69	51 Antimony (Sb) 121.75	52 Tellurium (Te) 127.60	53 Iodine (I) 126.904	54 Xenon (Xe) 131.30
64 adolinium) 157.25	65 Terbium (Tb) 158.924	66 Dysprosium (Dy) 162.50	67 Holmium (Ho) 164.930	68 Erbium (Er) 167.26	69 Thulium (Tm) 168.934	70 Ytterbium (Yb) 173.04	71 Lutetium (Lu) 174.97	
78 Platinum 195.09	79 Gold (Au) 196.967	80 Mercury (Hg) 200.59	81 Thallium (Tl) 204.37	82 Lead (Pb) 207.19	83 Bismuth (Bi) 208.98	84 Polonium (Po) 210.	85 Astatine (At) 210.	86 Radon (Rn) 222.
96 Curium m) 244.	97 Berkelium (Bk) 245.	98 Californium (Cf) 246.	99 Einsteinium (Es) 253.	100 Fermium (Fm) 255.	101 Mendelevium (Md) 256.	102 Nobelium (No) 255.	103 Lawrencium (Lr) 257	

families, or groups. With the heavier elements ten rows became necessary instead of seven, but the periodic repetition of properties still occurred. His table, which is still used today, is called "the periodic table of the elements." (See Table 1.)

Mendeleev found that to fit each element into its proper column, it was necessary at times to leave some places in the table blank. He predicted that elements would be found that belonged in these gaps and even described the properties that three of them would have. Several years later these three were discovered. They had almost precisely the properties that Mendeleev predicted. They were gallium, scandium, and germanium, all named after the countries of their discoverers.

Still, despite all of this information, no one knew what an atom was. Most scientists of the nineteenth century believed that an atom was indivisible, that it was an elementary particle. If this was true, the atom would have no internal structure and no parts, and would then be the building block of all the matter in the universe. However, in 1897 experiments in the field of electricity began to show that the atom could not qualify for such a role. It was far more complex. Like an onion, matter proved to be many-layered. Peeling the "compound" layer revealed the elements; beneath the elements lay the atoms. Now the atom layer was being peeled away.

2

Raisins in the Pudding

ABOUT 600 B.C. the Greek philosopher Thales of Miletus discovered that when he rubbed a piece of amber with some fur it attracted bits of feathers and other very light objects. He probably was one of the first to discover what later became known as "electricity." In fact, the word "electricity" was derived from the Greek word for amber, which is "elektron."

Many centuries later the study of electricity proved to be the key that began to unlock the mysteries of the atom. By the early seventeenth century it was known that glass also gains electrical properties if it is rubbed with fur. More than one hundred years later it was found that although two electrified amber rods repel each other, as do two electrified glass rods, an electrified amber rod and an electrified glass rod attract each other and lose their electricity if they are allowed to touch. Benjamin Franklin, who was not only a great statesman of his day but also an important scientist, suggested that the glass became "positively charged" when it was rubbed because electricity flowed into it as a sort of liquid. In a similar way, he said, electricity flowed out of the amber when it was rubbed, making it "negatively charged." Touching the two rods to each other allowed the electric fluid to flow from the positive to the negative achieving a neutral balance once again. We know now that the direction of the flow is reversed and that electricity is not a fluid, but otherwise Franklin's idea was a correct one.

To eighteenth-century scientists electricity represented a new form of energy that, it was believed, could be harnessed for many uses. With this incentive, plus the stimulation from Franklin's discoveries as well as others, experimentation with electricity—both as it is found in nature and as created in the laboratory—increased. Scientists performed just about every test they could think of in an attempt to find out more about this energy source. By the early ninteenth century the first electric batteries were built to produce a steady electric current. Then scientists no longer had to rely upon a temporary phenomenon, such as lightning or the "static electricity" obtained by rubbing objects, for their experiments.

At the same time, many tests were being performed with magnetism. Compasses had been in use in Europe since the twelfth century, having possibly come from the Chinese via the Arabs, but not much was known about why this invention worked or what this strange magnetic property really was. Once electricity started being investigated, however, its link with magnetism emerged. It was found, for example, that a cylindrical coil of wire behaves like a bar magnet if an electric current is made to flow through it. Such a current was able to move a compass needle, causing it to point away from the north magnetic pole. Then in 1831 the English scientist Michael Faraday discovered that by moving a magnet in and out of a coil of wire an electric current is generated in the wire. Faraday's discoveries led to the invention of electrical dynamos to generate electricity. Judging from our dependence today upon electricity, his findings changed human history.

In 1860 the English physicist James Clark Maxwell used the results of all the experiments performed with both magnetism and electricity to present a set of four equations. These showed mathematically the relationship between electricity

The English physicist James Clark Maxwell described the relationship between electricity and magnetism in terms of "fields."

and magnetism and demonstrated that they should not be thought of separately.

Maxwell described this relationship in terms of "fields," which, according to scientists, are regions of space within which some force, such as magnetism or electricity, is felt. Wherever a magnetic field existed, Maxwell said, an electric field had to be there at right angles to it. Together they formed an "electromagnetic field" around their source. Any change in either the electric or magnetic field produced a change in the other one, which in turn changed the first one again. This continual fluctuation caused the electromagnetic field to move outward from its source in all directions like the ripples on the surface of a pond after a rock has been thrown into it. Maxwell called the outward motion of this field "elec-

Figure 1. THE LENGTH OF AN ELECTROMAGNETIC WAVE

The length of the electromagnetic wave determines the type of radiation that reaches us.

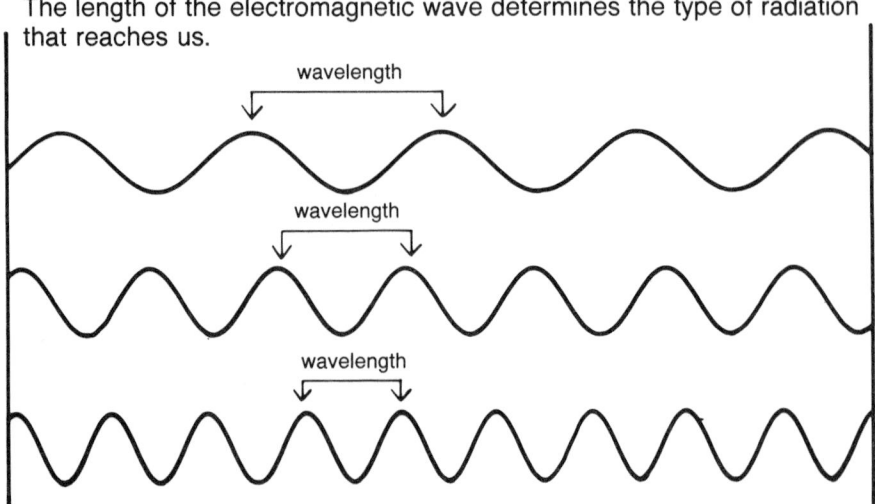

Length of wave is the distance between the crests.

tromagnetic radiation." Its "ripples," or "frequency," depended upon how rapidly the electromagnetic field itself waxed and waned. As you can see in Figure 1, the size of each wave, its "wavelength," is the distance from one crest or high point to the next. Some wavelengths are very short; others are much longer. All wavelengths are possible. All frequencies are possible.

When Maxwell calculated the speed of these electromagnetic waves, he found that regardless of their size or frequency, they always had exactly the same velocity as visible light. He inferred from these calculations that light was really a form of electromagnetic radiation. Although at that time light was the only type of radiation recognized as being electromagnetic, Maxwell went further and predicted that there was a much larger spectrum of electromagnetic energy waiting to be found. The only difference, he said, would be in the length of the electromagnetic wave and its frequency.

In 1887 radio waves were detected as another type of electromagnetic radiation. Unfortunately, Maxwell didn't live to see this discovery, which was a confirmation of his theory. Since then scientists have found many more forms of electromagnetic radiation, as Maxwell predicted. From Figure 2 you can see that visible light is only a very small portion of the total spectrum.

Figure 2. ELECTROMAGNETIC SPECTRUM

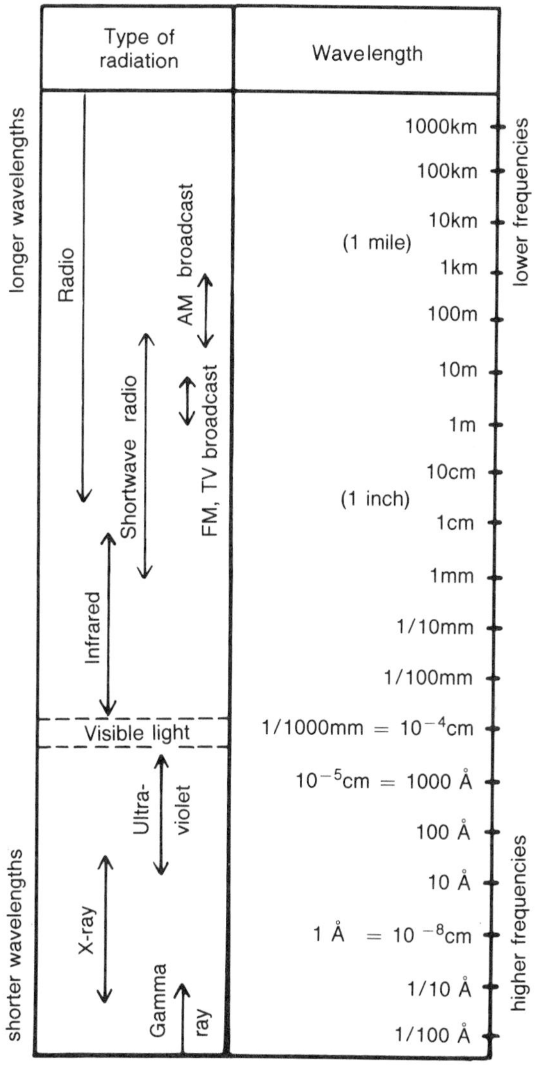

Type of radiation	Wavelength
longer wavelengths — Radio — Shortwave radio — AM broadcast — FM, TV broadcast — Infrared — Visible light — Ultra-violet — X-ray — Gamma ray — shorter wavelengths	1000km — 100km — 10km (1 mile) — 1km — 100m — 10m — 1m — 10cm (1 inch) — 1cm — 1mm — 1/10mm — 1/100mm — $1/1000mm = 10^{-4}cm$ — $10^{-5}cm = 1000 Å$ — 100 Å — 10 Å — $1 Å = 10^{-8}cm$ — 1/10 Å — 1/100 Å — lower frequencies ... higher frequencies

We now know that all electromagnetic radiation travels at the speed of light. As Maxwell hypothesized, it is the wavelength and frequency of each type of radiation that determines how we will perceive it. The longer the wavelength, the lower the frequency and vice versa. Thus, fewer radio waves will pass a given point each second than the much shorter X-rays.

Maxwell's equations, and experiments by others, were a big step forward in understanding electric and magnetic forces, but physicists and chemists still didn't know where these forces came from or what they were. There remained questions such as: If it wasn't a liquid that flowed between the electrified glass and amber rods, what was it? When an electric current was generated with the use of wire coils and magnets, what was happening? What was electricity?

One experiment gave a clue. It was originally attempted by Faraday as one of the numerous experiments he performed with electricity. He wanted to send an electric discharge through a vacuum rather than through an air-filled container. But Faraday could not produce a good enough vacuum, and the experiment had to wait until the middle of the nineteenth century when vacuum pumps were improved. Then, an adequate glass vacuum tube was produced with a wire implanted in it through which an electric current could be sent. Faraday had called this wire the "cathode," or negative pole. With the improved vacuum tubes, whenever a current was introduced through the cathode, a green glow appeared on the tube wall opposite the cathode.

Because the green glow appeared to emanate from the cathode, it was called a "cathode ray." However, there was great controversy at first as to what cathode rays were. Some scientists believed they were a form of electromagnetic radiation. Others said they were a flow of particles of some kind. If they were particles, it was assumed that they were electrically charged since they were the product of an electric current.

These experimenters already knew that when electrically charged particles are brought close to the pole of a battery, they are either attracted toward the pole or repelled from it. The reaction depends upon whether the particles and pole are of opposite signs (which causes them to be attracted to each other) or of the same sign (which causes repulsion). These reactions are similar to those obtained by earlier experiments using amber and glass rods.

At that time scientists also knew that a magnet will affect charged particles in motion in a similar way: It will change the particles' direction depending upon the sign of the pole. Electromagnetic radiation, however, is not affected in this way by either electrical or magnetic charges. Therefore, these charges could be used to determine whether the mysterious cathode rays were electromagnetic radiation or particles.

In 1897 the physicist Joseph John Thomson demonstrated that the cathode rays were deflected by electric charges. In his experiments, when either the pole of a battery or a magnet was brought close to the vacuum tube, the green glow moved away from its former position. The direction of its deflection depended upon whether an attractive or repulsive reaction was taking place. This proved that the cathode rays were not radiation but were composed of electrically charged particles streaming from the cathode to the "anode," or positive, pole. Because of their electrical origin, these particles were called "electrons." And because they came from the cathode, or negative, pole, they were said to have a negative electric charge.

But where did these electrons come from? Did they come from the atoms that made up the cathode wire? If that was so, the atom was not indivisible as scientists had previously

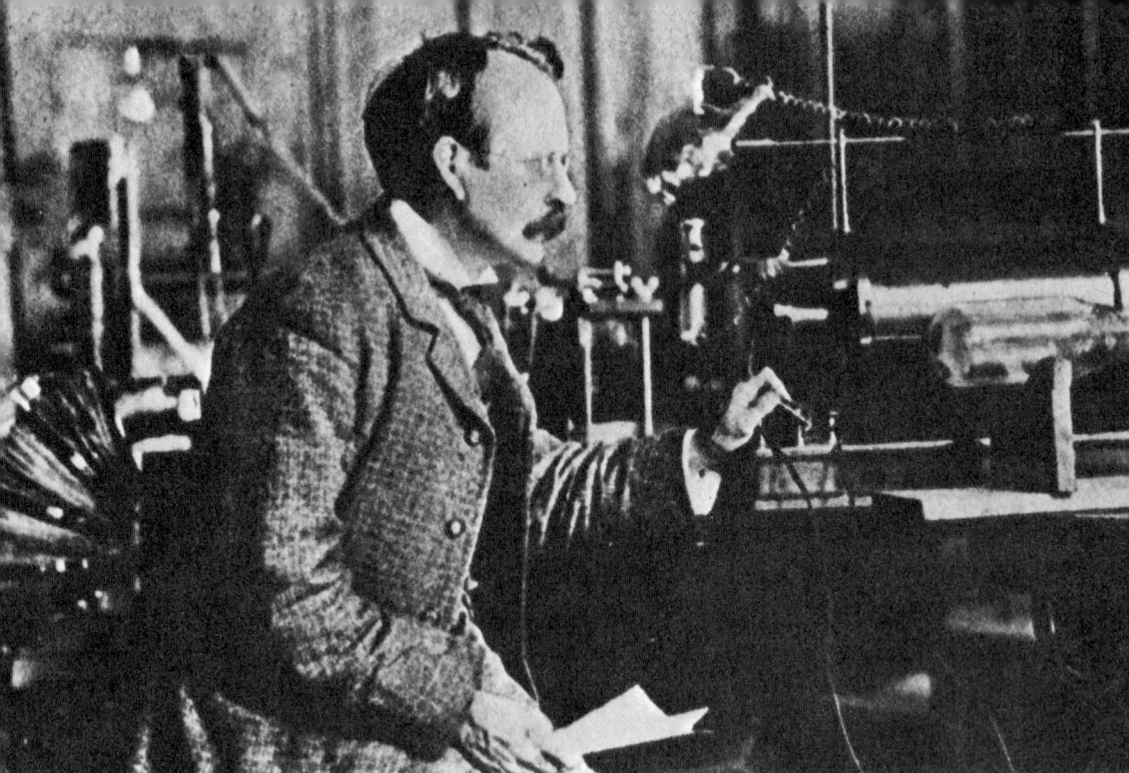

Fermilab. Joseph John Thomson's experiments with cathode rays demonstrated that they were composed of electrically charged particles.

thought. For electrons to come out of atoms, the atom must have an internal structure—it must have parts to it. Because scientists knew the atom itself has no electrical charge (it is neutral), this also meant that somewhere inside the atom there was a positively charged section that neutralized the negative charge of the electron.

These were not easy ideas for many physicists and chemists to accept after having considered the atom an elementary and indivisible particle for so long a time. There were some, however, who suspected that the atom was not the final core of the onion; and when the electron was discovered, these same people suggested the possibility that it was part of the atom.

Then in 1900 an experiment by the German physicist Philipp Lenard revealed that electrons were emitted from the surface of certain metals when a strong beam of light was shined upon them. These metals then acquired a positive charge. When other physicists began to experiment with this phenomenon, which became known as the "photoelectric effect," they found that by changing the wavelength of the light, they could change the energy and velocity of the emitted electrons. This change did not occur when they merely altered the brightness of the light beam. The greater intensity kicked out more electrons from the surface of the metal, but the energy of the electrons as they left the metal stayed the same. Blue light was found to give the electrons much more energy than yellow light, but ultraviolet light was even more powerful.

Although Lenard was awarded the Nobel Prize in 1905 for the discovery of the photoelectric effect, it was the famous physicist Albert Einstein who explained why the effect occurred. A beam of light consists of many rays. When each

The deflection vacuum tube used by Joseph John Thomson at Cavendish Laboratory in his studies of cathode rays.
History of Astronomy Collection, Price Photographic Archive, Adler Planetarium.

light ray hits the metal, Einstein said, its force pushes an electron out of an atom in the metal. The amount of energy the light ray has depends upon its wavelength; for instance, the shorter waves at the blue end of the spectrum are most energetic. Increasing the intensity of the light merely adds more light rays to the beam, causing more electrons to be ejected. But it does not give those electrons any more energy than the dimmer beam gives them. Einstein was awarded the Nobel Prize in 1921 for his explanation of this phenomenon. Today it is used extensively in "electric eyes" that automatically open and close doors at many entranceways and elevators.

The electrons emitted in the photoelectric effect were found to be identical to those making up the cathode rays. This discovery helped to finally remove any lingering doubt about the electrons' source. Clearly, they had come from the atoms themselves. This meant that the atom was not an elementary particle—it did have an internal structure and could be broken into smaller parts.

Still, scientists did not know where these parts were within the atom. Where were the electrons and where was the positively charged part, whatever it might be? Thomson suggested that they were somehow embedded in the atomic material, as shown in Figure 3, like so many raisins in a

Figure 3   RAISINS IN THE PUDDING

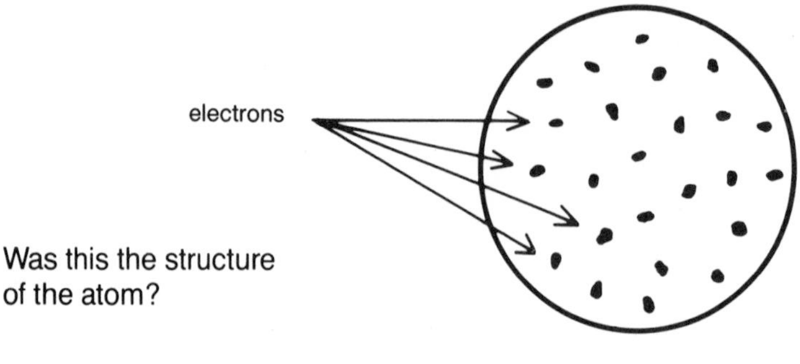

electrons

Was this the structure
of the atom?

pudding, but no one knew what the rest of the pudding was like.

This was the picture that scientists had of the atom as the twentieth century began. During the next eighty years more was learned about atomic structure and elementary particles than in all the preceding centuries. In the course of this work, a new branch of physics—particle physics—developed, which was based upon two major theories presented early in the century. These were Einstein's theory of relativity and the quantum theory. Eventually the scope of these theories encompassed the entire universe from the very smallest particle to the largest cluster of galaxies.

As new research tools and methods were developed to deal with the increasingly complex discoveries, astronomers, chemists, and physicists all became involved. Today teams of scientists undertake most research projects because they are too expensive and too difficult for one person to handle alone. Also, frequent contact with others in the field is necessary to keep up with current advances, and collaboration with others either in the same lab or in other parts of the world is essential for much of the investigative work.

This cooperative effort requires that scientists go to several meetings and workshops throughout the year to exchange ideas, debate new ones, and question their colleagues on their latest findings. They also keep themselves and others up to date by circulating "preprints," which are copies of pre-publication research papers reporting the newest findings. Many months later these papers will appear in scientific journals but by then the projects may be far ahead, investigating new avenues or designing better experiments.

Both experimental and theoretical physicists (as well as other scientists) are involved in these meetings, workshops, and preprint exchanges. Theorists try to explain the way nature works, whereas experimenters design tests to observe how nature works. The theorist's description may at first be in normal language but eventually it must be presented mathematically. It must be precise if it is to be scientifically sound. Not all hypotheses lead to positive results. Stacks of paper filled with formulae and calculations representing weeks or even months of work may wind up at a dead end. But sometimes even these may show the way to another possible answer—and the process starts again.

Experimental physicists take the theorists' hypotheses and attempt to confirm or refute them. They must design tests that will enable them to observe and measure some aspect of the natural world. The results of these experiments, especially if they refute the proposed theory, send theorists back to the "drawing board" for new ideas or for the refinement of older ones. In this way the two groups of scientists work together, each contributing their expertise.

In this book many people are cited for their scientific work, especially Nobel Prize winners. But because so many scientists contribute to a given research project, it is often difficult, if not impossible, to reward any one person for an achievement. (This is one problem the Nobel Prize committee as well as other award-giving organizations encounter.) We should remember, therefore, what Isaac Newton said when praised for his scientific genius: "If I have seen farther than others, it is because I have stood on the shoulders of giants."

3

The Peach Pit Nucleus

How do you find out about the inside of an object that is so tiny it can't be seen even through a powerful microscope? This was the problem confronting physicists at the beginning of the twentieth century. How could they explore the inside of the atom? One possibility was to poke it with something even smaller, if such an object could be found. It would be like trying to find out about the inside of a piece of fruit by sticking a long, thin needle into different parts of its skin. With enough of these probes, you would learn, for example, that a peach has a large pit at its center, whereas a watermelon has many smaller pits scattered about.

But what is smaller than an atom? What could be used as a "needle" probe? The answer came from experiments that were conducted with "radioactive" elements. The name radioactive comes from a description of these elements' "ray-giving activity," and was suggested by Marie Curie, the Polish-born scientist who pioneered the investigation into this field, and who was awarded the Nobel Prize in 1903 and 1911 for her discoveries.

Radioactive elements, such as uranium and radium, spontaneously emit a strange kind of radiation. They don't need to have their atoms excited by an electric current or bombarded by light rays. The emission is a natural occurrence. However, not all the radiation coming from these special

One of the leaders in radioactive research at the turn of the century was the English physicist Ernest Rutherford.

substances is the same. Much of it was found to be tiny particles that are continuously emitted, like tiny bullets, from the elements' atoms. Scientists soon realized that these emissions could be used as the "needles" to probe the atomic "fruit."

Ernest Rutherford, an English physicist, was one of the leaders in this radioactive research. In fact, he received the Nobel Prize in 1908 for his work in this field. In some of his experiments in the early 1900s, he aimed radioactive particles at a very thin sheet of gold or platinum foil. Although solid in appearance and capable of stopping ordinary visible light, the metal foil could be pierced by the tiny radioactive particles because they moved with so strong a thrust. To use our analogy of the peach and watermelon, in order to probe the interior of the fruit, a certain amount of force is necessary for the needle to pierce the skin. Gently tapping it with the point is not sufficient. Similarly, a normal ray of visible light is too weak to pierce the metal foil, whereas the rapidly moving radioactive particles are energetic enough to do so.

Figure 4. RUTHERFORD'S EXPERIMENT

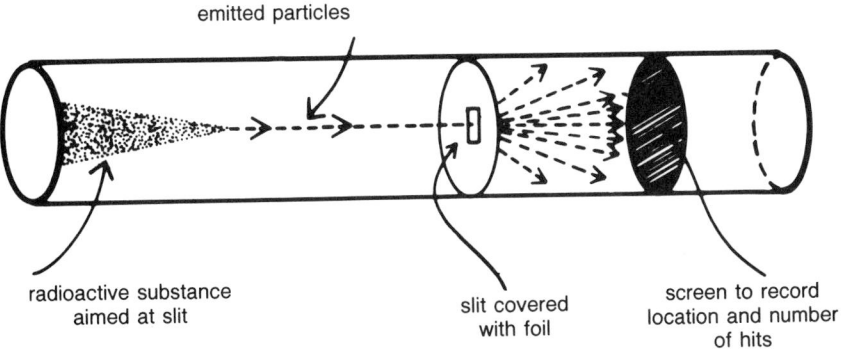

emitted particles

radioactive substance aimed at slit

slit covered with foil

screen to record location and number of hits

On the other side of the foil Rutherford put a sheet of photographic film. When each particle went through the foil and struck the film, it produced a mark where it landed. (See Figure 4.) After developing the film, researchers were able to determine from the photographs how many particles went through the sheet of metal and what their paths had been.

The "raisins in the pudding" model of the atom implied that the mass of the atom was spread out evenly throughout its volume. Electrons were already known to be very light particles, contributing extremely little to the atomic mass. Because they were so easily removed from the atom, they were assumed to be located somewhere in its outer part.

In Rutherford's experiments, the raisins-in-the-pudding hypothesis lead to the prediction that high-velocity radioactive particles would go right through the foil and continue in a straight line until they hit the film. This would be because the electrons were too small and the spread-out material of the rest of the atom too thin to stop the particles or alter their paths in any way. It would be like firing a round of BB's into a loose bunch of cotton balls or feathers.

But this is not what happened. From the photographs it was evident that the great majority—but not all—of the particles did pass straight through the foil and were not deflected from their paths. However, some were noticeably deflected to one side or the other; their paths had been changed. They had hit something while going through the foil and had bounced off of it into another direction, much like a collision of two billiard balls. (See Figure 5.) From the pattern that the scattered particles left on the film, Rutherford determined that the "something" they had hit must be hard and impenetrable, not at all like fluffy cotton balls or feathers.

He realized from previous experiments that the electrons in the atoms were not big enough to have been able to cause such an effect. Therefore, he hypothesized that the deflected particles must have hit a much denser and larger concentration of matter located somewhere within the atom. He called this concentration the atomic "nucleus." According to his model of the atom, the nucleus was where practically all the atomic mass was located. Only the tiny electrons were outside of it.

Figure 5. SCATTERING OF PARTICLES GOING THROUGH GOLD FOIL

Most particles were not scattered as indicated by the peak of the curve at the 0.00 point.

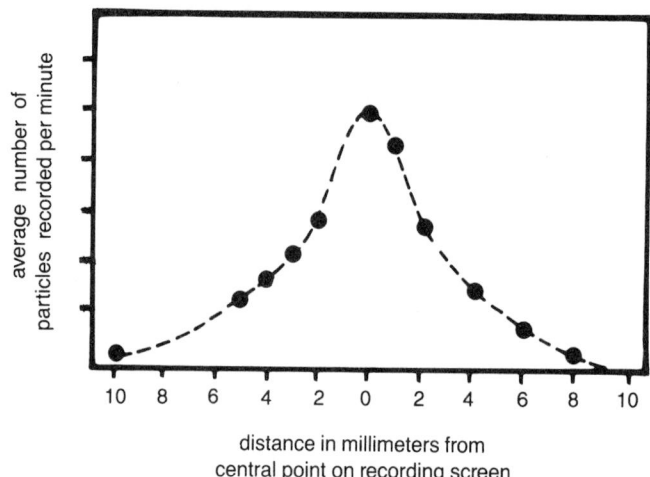

distance in millimeters from
central point on recording screen

Rutherford knew that hydrogen was the lightest element and he therefore assumed that its nucleus was made up of a single particle. He called this particle the "proton" from the Greek word "protos" for "first." The proton had actually been detected but not recognized as the hydrogen nucleus by the German physicist Eugen Goldstein in 1886. In experiments with radiation going through cathode ray tubes, Goldstein found a new radiation streaming in the opposite direction to the negatively charged cathode rays and called it "channel rays." Later experiments proved that like the cathode rays, channel rays were actually streams of charged particles, except that in this case they were considered positively charged because they moved in an opposite direction to the stream of electrons. Each channel particle was found to carry a charge equal but opposite to that of the electron.

It was Rutherford who recognized that a channel ray particle is the same as the single particle that makes up the hydrogen nucleus. He envisioned this nucleus to be at the center of the atom, with its positive charge offset by a single electron circling around it. In heavier atoms he pictured the protons all crowded together in a compact central mass, with an orbiting electron in the outer regions of the atom for every proton in the nucleus. The location of the electrons was surmised from the ease with which they could be removed from the atom. It was believed that if they were located in the nucleus, they would not be so easily detachable.

Rutherford was correct in stating that the nucleus contains practically all the atom's mass. The proton is now known to be 1,836 times as massive as the electron. However, it has a diameter of only about one hundred-thousandth that of the entire atom. Also, the concept of orbiting electrons was found to be a false representation of their activity, which is far more complicated. However, this model is still used as a convenient way of describing atomic structure.

The proton, then, was the long sought-after part of the atom that offset the electron and made the atom neutral. In Rutherford's day, both of these atomic particles, the electron and proton, were considered to be elementary particles. It was believed that they were indivisible and could have no parts. Scientists did find it strange, however, for such a massive particle, the proton, to have the same charge as the tiny electron. This did not seem the kind of balance and simplicity that appears to exist in nature and that scientists are continually looking for. The reason for this gross disparity is still not completely clear.

The "atomic number" of an element in Mendeleev's periodic table now took on more meaning. It represented the number of electrons or protons in each atom of any given element. As you know, there has to be an equal number of both particles if the atom is to be neutrally charged, and the greater the number of particles, the more massive the atom. This mass is the "atomic weight." From Table 1 on pages 18–19, you can see how both the number and weight increase as you go up Mendeleev's table. For example, helium is the second lightest element. Its atomic number is 2. Like hydrogen, it is also a gas in its normal state here on earth. It is so light that helium-filled balloons quickly fly up into the sky and disappear from sight. (Hydrogen-filled balloons would do the same thing, but because hydrogen is dangerously combustible, helium is more frequently used in balloons instead.)

The helium atom has two electrons and two protons. However, you will note from the table that its atomic weight is about 4.003, about four times that of hydrogen. How can that be? With twice as many protons, its weight should only be twice as great, not four times. Going up the table to heavier and heavier elements, you will notice that this discrepancy becomes even greater. An iron atom, for example, with an atomic number of 26, has an atomic weight of 55.847, almost fifty-six times heavier than a hydrogen atom. Since the weight of the electrons is negligible and the protons contribute only about twenty-six times the hydrogen atom's weight, where does the rest of the weight come from?

Rutherford hypothesized that another particle in the nucleus was responsible. Because it would have to be electrically neutral so as not to upset the atom's neutrality, it was called a "neutron." But it wasn't until 1932 that the English physicist James Chadwick actually proved experimentally the existence of Rutherford's hypothetical particle. The neutron was found to have about the same mass as the proton but it was neutrally charged.

When the existence of the neutron was confirmed, the extra weight in the atomic nuclei became clear. The helium atom was found to have two electrons, two protons, and two neutrons. The protons and the neutrons make it four times heavier than the hydrogen atom with its one proton and one electron. (Hydrogen is the only element that has no neutrons in its nucleus.) Heavier nuclei have far more neutrons than the helium nucleus and many contain more neutrons than protons. Because the neutron is neutrally charged, these extra neutrons do not affect the atom's overall charge.

The atomic model presented by Rutherford and others after the discovery of the neutron consisted of three major particles. These particles were all believed to be indivisible and therefore elementary. It was found from many experiments that all protons are identical. The same is true of neutrons and electrons. The differences between different kinds of atoms and the elements they make up lies in the number and the arrangements of these particles. The atomic number of an element defines how many protons it has in its nucleus, but the atomic weight is the sum of all its protons and neutrons.

Before we delve deeper into the structure of the atom, let us pause to consider its size. Democritus would have been astounded to learn that ten million atoms could be placed on the period at the end of this sentence. One atom is about 10^{-8} centimeter in diameter (a centimeter is about one-third inch).

If we enlarge an atom a quadrillion times (10^{15}), it will be about sixty miles in diameter. At its center we will find a small hard sphere the size of a soccer ball. That's the nucleus. Flying around the soccer ball at various distances tens of miles from it are many tiny marbles that represent the electrons. All the rest of this fantasy is empty space. It is no wonder that such a picture of the atom was unbelievable to many people. This book appears to be a solid object. So do most other things that we touch. They are all made of atoms. How can they be mostly empty space? As we will see later, this space is not really empty, but what it does contain is even more astounding.

The Secret of Light

As NINETEENTH-CENTURY PHYSICISTS learned more about the newly discovered components of the atom and about the equally new forms of electromagnetic radiation, they began to find these two fields of research interrelated. To understand their relationship to each other, we must first go back to the seventeenth century when the famous English scientist Sir Isaac Newton was investigating the nature of light. Maxwell's equations were still more than a hundred years in the future and very little was known about the origin or cause of light. Some scientists believed it was a stream of tiny particles; others thought that it was a wave phenomenon. However, Newton was one of the first to conduct serious experiments to determine what light really was.

In one of his experiments, Newton allowed a beam of sunlight to shine through a glass prism. This caused the beam to be spread out into a rainbow band that was called a "spectrum" after the Greek word for "ghost." (See Figure 6.) Using a second prism, Newton found he could recombine the spectrum of colors into the original narrow, colorless beam of light. He correctly theorized that ordinary light, such as sunlight, is really a combination of all the colors of the rainbow and that the prism is able to spread out this light by "refracting," or bending, each color at a slightly different angle. Then color rays no longer all travel in the same direc-

Figure 6. NEWTON'S EXPERIMENT

Each color is bent or refracted at a different angle, creating a spectrum. Blue and violet light are bent the most; red, the least.

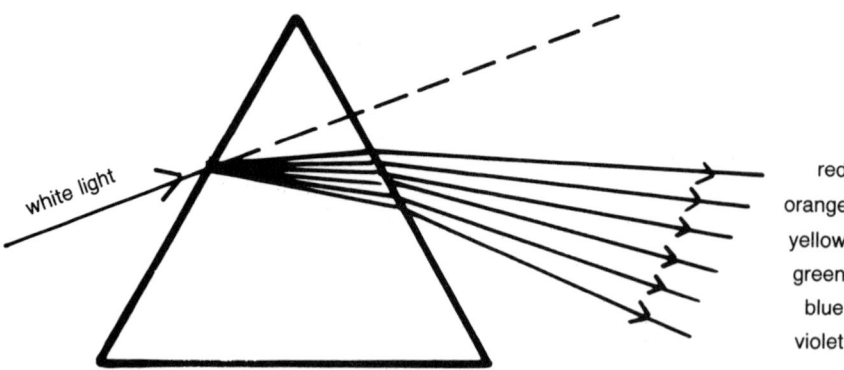

tion until they are recombined with the second prism.

Newton experimented further with light, especially noting that it always seemed to travel in straight lines and cast sharp shadows when it hit opaque objects. He concluded from all his research that since light could not go around these objects or around any corners, it was not like water waves, which can easily flow around a log in their path. Instead, he said, light must be a stream of rapidly moving tiny particles, which he called "corpuscles." He could not explain, however, why these corpuscles never hit each other when two light beams crossed each other.

Later in the same century, Christian Huygens, a Dutch physicist, rejected Newton's particle theory of light. He declared that his experiments showed light to be made up of tiny waves, not particles. These waves were different lengths, he said, and that determined how much they were refracted when passing through the prism. His experiments demonstrated that violet and blue light waves are refracted the most and have the shortest wavelengths; the longest waves are those of red light, which is refracted the least. In between these two extremes are all the other colors of the rainbow.

Huygens's wave theory was able to explain how two beams of light could cross each other without difficulty. If you throw two rocks into a pond, the ripples of water will crisscross each other as they expand outward. Huygens's wave theory pictured light rays behaving in the same manner. However, it also had its drawbacks. One of Newton's criticisms was that it failed to explain how light could travel across the great expanses of empty space. Water waves require water to move through; sound waves need air or some other conductor. If starlight was a wave, what was it moving through? What was it waving in? How did it reach us?

Both Newton's and Huygens's theories had their supporters, but Newton's particle theory was more widely accepted by other scientists and was the dominant one throughout the eighteenth century. This was due primarily to the high esteem in which this great man was held by his colleagues.

Then, in 1801, Thomas Young, an English physicist, performed an experiment that changed this picture. A narrow beam of light was focused on two closely spaced slits in a screen. A second screen was placed behind the first one. The resulting "interference pattern" on the second screen could only be explained by the wave theory of light. You will learn more about these experiments in the next chapter. From these results, however, Young was able to measure the actual size of a light wave. He found that red light was 0.000075 centimeter in length and violet light, 0.000039 centimeter. Today we use a unit of measure called an "angstrom" (Å), which is one hundred-millionth (10^{-8} or 0.00000001) of a centimeter. Thus, red light has a wavelength of 7500 Å and violet light a wavelength of 3900 Å.

Once the minute size of light waves had been determined, physicists understood why light always seemed to cast sharp shadows and never go around corners. The human-scale objects that had been used in the experiments were a hundred thousand times larger than any light waves. If an object thousands of times longer than an ocean wave is placed on the surface of the ocean, it will effectively stop any wave motion. Only at either end will there still be some disturbance. For example, small waves hitting the side of a large ship are stopped and the water on the opposite side of the ship is much smoother. (See Figure 7.)

In the same way, a light wave may be stopped by your finger, causing a sharp shadow to be cast, or it may be very slightly bent, causing a more fuzzy one to appear. Like the large ship in the water, your finger is thousands of times larger than any light wave. But if a light wave encounters a submicroscopic particle that is about its own size, it will easily curve around it just like water waves move almost undisturbed around a tiny stick. This is yet another example of how the submicroscopic world is so different from our ordinary one.

Is light, then, a stream of particles or is it a wave phenomenon? Strange as it may seem, it is both. There are some experiments that show its particle nature and others that show its wavelike nature. Either way, as James Clark Maxwell said in 1860, light is electromagnetic radiation, the oscillation of electrical and magnetic fields radiating outward.

Here's an example of how this happens. If we put an iron poker into a roaring fire, it soon becomes hot enough to give off its own heat and eventually may even become "red hot," that is, it will emit a red glowing light.

Where does this light come from? How is it created? The iron rod absorbs energy from the fire and then emits it as

Figure 7. MICROSCOPIC VERSUS MACROSCOPIC

Ocean waves pass by a small log sticking out of the water, but they are greatly affected by a giant ocean liner that is much bigger than they are. In the same way, light waves will be stopped by your finger but can easily go around a subatomic particle.

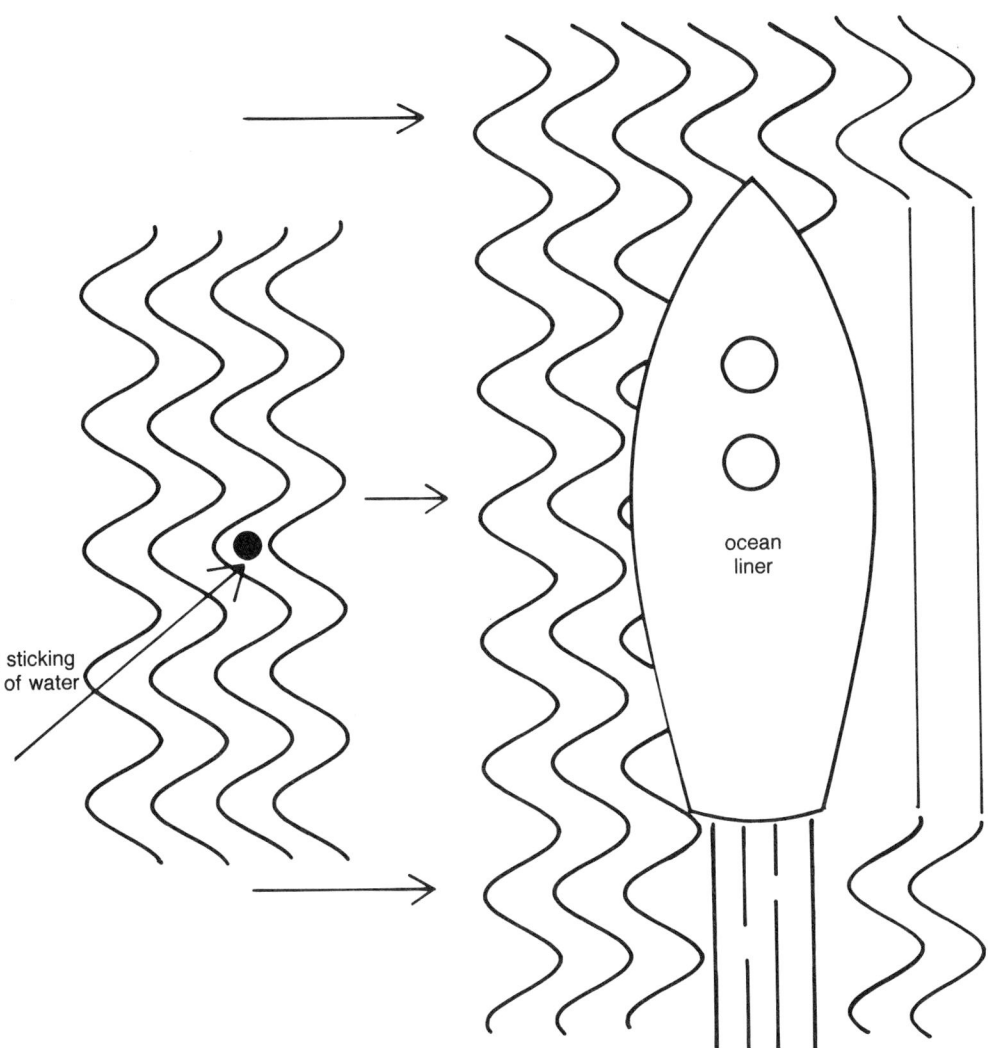

heat and light. In this case, both of these are forms of electromagnetic radiation, each with its own wavelength.

If we heat the iron further, it will turn bright red, then orange, and possibly even yellowish as its temperature rises. The wavelength of its radiation will grow shorter and shorter because, as you can see in Figure 2 on page 25, yellow light has a shorter wavelength than red.

In other words, the shorter the wavelength, the more energy the radiation has. The formula for calculating the exact amount of energy radiated from an object at each wavelength was presented by the German physicist Max Planck in 1900. He found, however, that his formula would not work unless an entirely new concept of energy was adopted. Radiation, he said, is not a continuous flow of energy as had been assumed previously, but, like matter, it is made up of tiny units. The continuous flow of energy that we observe, according to this theory, is caused by our own inability to distinguish these individual units. Planck called each unit a "quantum" from the Latin word for "how much." This was the introduction of the quantum theory, for which Planck received the Nobel Prize in 1918. At first it was not accepted by other physicists, but five years later Albert Einstein used Planck's theory to explain the reason for the photoelectric effect, which could not be explained by the old theories of light. Along with the theory of relativity, the quantum theory was to revolutionize twentieth-century science.

According to the quantum theory, each quantum has a specific amount of energy, which depends upon the wavelength of its radiation. The shorter the wavelength, the greater the quantum's energy. Blue light has more energy than red light. Gamma rays are much more energetic than radio waves. It takes more energy to produce a glowing red poker than one that just gives off heat but no light. The seemingly smooth flow of heat and light that we receive from the red-hot iron poker is not really continuous and undivided but rather a series of tiny packets, or quanta, of energy. It is energy in the form of radiation that is emitted by the individual atoms in the iron. To see how, let us go back to the early models of the atom after the nucleus was discovered. The most famous one was presented by Niels Bohr, a Danish physicist. For his work he received the Nobel Prize in 1922.

The Bohr model showed a central nucleus with electrons orbiting around it. (See Figure 8.) The electrons were arranged in "shells," or concentric orbits, and for each orbiting electron there was a proton within the nucleus. Unlike the planets in the solar system, there could be more than one electron orbiting at each shell, and each electron could jump from one orbit to another, up or down.

When we heat an iron poker, the atoms in it absorb energy from the fire. We say that the atoms in the iron are in an "excited state." When that happens, some of the electrons in each iron atom are raised to higher energy levels, which means they jump up to larger orbits. The more energy the atom absorbs, the larger each electron's orbit may become.

However, the electron does not stay at the higher orbit, or higher energy level, very long. Within perhaps one hundred-millionth of a second it jumps back down to a lower level and emits some or all of the energy it just absorbed. These jumps up or down in energy levels are very specific quantities—only certain jumps can take place; only specific amounts of energy can be emitted; only certain orbits can be occupied. For each chemical element there is a series of such energy levels which the electrons in that element's atoms can jump up to and come down from. The more energy the atom absorbs, the higher the electron can jump. Sometimes an electron is able to jump up or down more than one level but it must always

Figure 8. THE BOHR MODEL OF THE ATOMS OF THREE ELEMENTS

Electrons do not actually orbit the nucleus; their positions at any time cannot be accurately known. (Note that neither the size of the particles nor the size of the orbits is drawn to scale.)

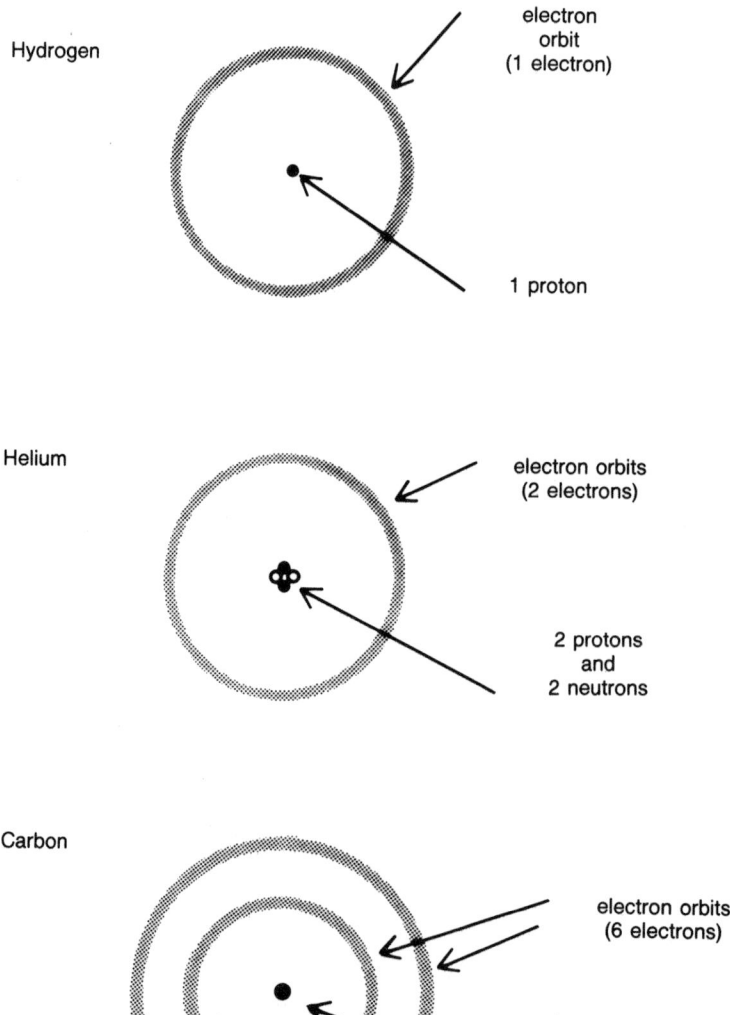

Hydrogen

electron
orbit
(1 electron)

1 proton

Helium

electron orbits
(2 electrons)

2 protons
and
2 neutrons

Carbon

electron orbits
(6 electrons)

6 protons
and
6 neutrons

end up at an energy level allowed for that element. (See Figure 9.)

Bohr was able to determine the permitted orbits for the hydrogen atom's electron by first measuring the wavelength of the radiation that the hydrogen atoms absorbed or emitted. He could then calculate what size the orbits must be to agree with the measured wavelengths. Later, similar observations and calculations were made for other elements, but neither Bohr nor anyone else at that time could explain why nature permitted only these specific orbits.

According to Bohr, each time an electron jumps down to a lower energy level, it emits a quantum of energy, called a "photon." We cannot easily detect a photon that is emitted by a single electron without very special instruments, but

Figure 9. "PERMITTED" ELECTRON ORBITS

Once raised to a higher "permitted" orbit, the electron jumps back down to a lower one. It sometimes makes a series of jumps rather than one large one. With each jump, a photon of energy is emitted. This drawing does not represent any specific atom but rather is a schematic diagram of a hypothetical atom.

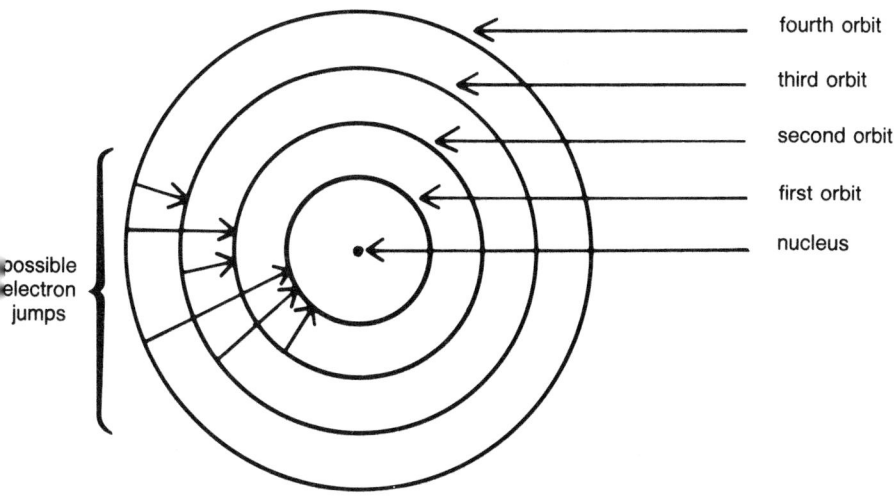

when millions and billions of atoms are all busy absorbing and emitting photons over and over again, we see or feel the collective effect—heat and light. To us it appears as a smooth and continuous flow because we cannot distinguish the individual quanta.

The highest energy photons are detected as gamma rays and X-rays while the lowest ones are radio and TV radiation. In the visible region of the electromagnetic spectrum, photons of blue light have the most energy and red, the least. In between these two extremes are the rest of the color spectrum.

This means that for every electromagnetic wavelength there is a corresponding photon of energy. The larger the electron jump, the greater the energy of the photon and smaller the wavelength of the radiation that is sent outward. In other words, each wave of electromagnetic radiation is made up of photons of specific energy.

Does this mean that both Newton and Huygens were correct? Yes and no. Neither of them really knew the true nature of light. Neither of them imagined it could have a wave-particle duality. It is not an easy concept to understand or accept, but many experiments and mathematical analyses have proven its validity. However, the photon is not the only particle that has a wave-particle duality. Roughly speaking, the quantum theory says that all matter is quantized; it is all discrete, individual particles. And all objects of every size share the duality of particle and wave, although it is easiest to demonstrate the wave phenomenon for the very lightest particles, such as photons and electrons. The wave property of electrons was an important discovery because it enabled scientists to develop the "electron microscope," which then allowed them to study much smaller objects than they could see with microscopes that use light. Let us look now at some of the experiments in which the electron exhibits wave characteristics rather than particle ones. These experiments will take us into another important aspect of the quantum theory —probability. As we will see, the search for elementary particles took an unexpected twist as physicists learned more about the quantum strata of matter.

What Are the Odds?

IN HIS QUANTUM THEORY, Max Planck hypothesized that electromagnetic radiation could have the characteristics of particles in the form of photons as well as those of waves. Then in 1923 Louis Victor de Broglie, a French physicist, theorized that particles such as electrons behaved like waves under certain conditions. He even was able to calculate that electrons traveling at moderate speeds would have wavelengths comparable to those of X-rays. Experiments soon proved his hypothesis to be correct and he received the Nobel Prize in 1929. Let us look at a simple experiment that demonstrates the electron's wavelike property. It is similar to the light wave experiment performed by Thomas Young in 1801.

A beam of electrons is aimed at a thick barrier with a screen on the opposite side. In the barrier are two tiny slits through which the electrons can pass. In order for the wavelike effect to be seen, these slits must be very close to one another compared to the electron's wavelength.

First only one slit is opened. Most of the electrons that pass through the opening will hit a point on the screen directly opposite the slit. A few may hit the sides of the slit and be slightly deflected so that they land on either side of this point. If we draw an intensity curve, which shows the distribution of the electron hits on the screen, it will look like the one in part D in Figure 10. If the first slit is closed and the second

THE PARTICLE-WAVE EXPERIMENT

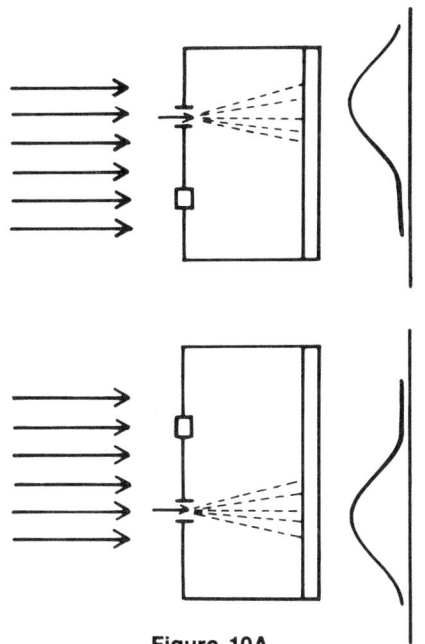

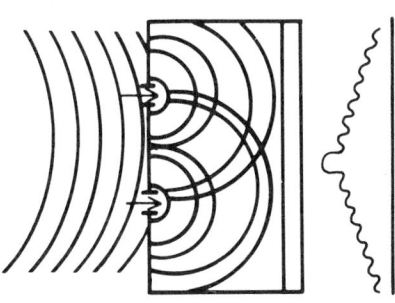

Figure 10A.

If BB's are fired at the apparatus with one or the other slot open, most hit a point on the screen directly opposite the slot.

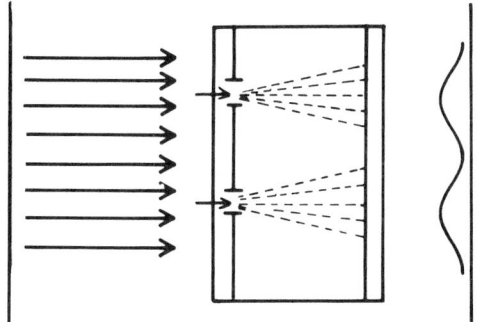

Figure 10B.

If both slots are open when the BB's are fired, the intensity curve will show two high points.

Figure 10D.

Electrons fired through the apparatus with one slot open act like particles.

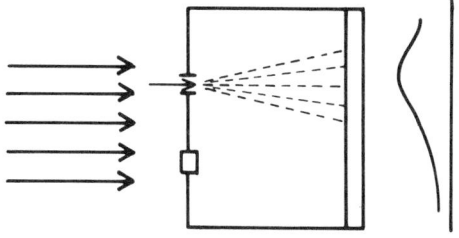

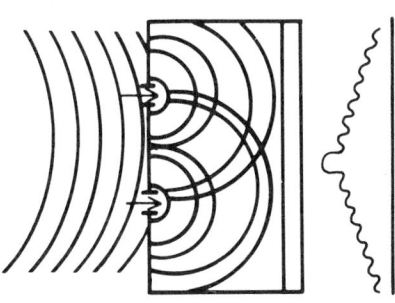

Figure 10C.

Water waves pushed against opened slots create overlapping waves on the other side, an interference effect.

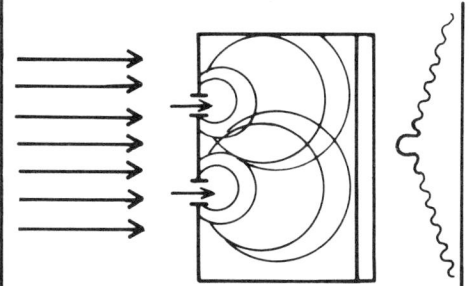

Figure 10E.

Electrons fired through the apparatus with two slots open act like waves.

one opened, the same curve will result, this time directly opposite the second slit. In this experiment the electrons are acting like particles. We would expect the same kind of intensity curve if we fired many rounds of BB's through small openings. (See part A in Figure 10.)

What happens if both slits are opened? Would we see two high points in the curve, one opposite each slit? That is what we would get if we allowed the BB's to go through either hole. But that doesn't happen with the electrons. (Compare parts B and E in Figure 10.) Instead, the intensity curve appears as a wiggly line with its highest point midway between the two slits. Why?

When both slits are open, the electrons exhibit wave rather than particle characteristics. We would get such a wiggly line if we sent waves of water through the two holes. (See part C in Figure 10.) Two sets of waves emerge from the other side and overlap each other. At some points this overlapping creates a larger overall wave whereas at other points the waves cancel each other out. The net effect is an uneven or wiggly intensity curve that indicates how high the wave is at each point when it reaches the wall (or screen). Such a pattern is caused by the "interference" of the two waves with each other. This same interference effect frequently occurs with sound waves, too. The intensity of the sound fluctuates as the two crossing sound waves interact with each other.

This is also what happens to electrons when both slits in the barrier are left open. Instead of maintaining their particle identity and acting like tiny BB's, they behave like waves. After emerging from the slits, the electron waves overlap each other and create interference patterns. The effect is the same kind of wiggly intensity curve as that caused by water waves.

In the case of water waves, the intensity curve tells us how high the wave was at any point. The height of the wave is a measure of how much water actually hit the screen at that point. With the electron wave, the curve tells us where the greatest number of electrons landed. Notice that the highest point on both curves is midway between the two slits.

From such information we can determine how likely it is, or the "probability," that an electron will hit the screen at any given point. Or, if you are a gambler, the "odds." The higher the curve at any particular point, the better the odds that an electron will hit the screen there.

In other words, when both slits are open, each electron is indeed a particle and can go through only one slit or the other. However, unlike the BB's, we cannot tell which slit any specific electron will go through. We can only calculate what the probability is that an electron will be detected at some specific point on the screen. How it gets from the source to the screen we can never know.

Why is this? Let us try to look at a specific electron as we might look at a BB. We can use fast speed photography to follow an individual BB from the gun to the target. What shall we use to view the electron with? Most of the information we have of the world around us comes from using light rays. But what happens when we shine a light upon our tiny electron? The force of the photons immediately changes the electron's position and course. If only one photon is capable of pushing an electron around, think of what a beam of them will do. The very act of measuring the electron's position will cause it to be changed. Our attempted measurement will be a certain failure. The result would be comparable to using a thick club to probe the inside of the peach in Chapter Three. We'd probably end up with peach puree and have no knowledge of where the pit had been.

This effect is not confined to only atomic particles. For

example, if you want to measure the air pressure in your
bicycle tires, the very act of attaching the gauge and remov-
ing it lets out a little air and reduces the pressure a tiny bit.
A cold thermometer placed into a roast in the oven will lower
slightly the temperature of the cooking meat as it registers its
internal heat.

These changes are very small and they can be overlooked
in performing everyday measurements. However, when we
attempt to measure individual subatomic particles, we can't
ignore such reactions because they are greater than any
measurements we may make.

This measuring reaction occurs in any research in which an
attempt to locate a specific electron (or any other subatomic
particle) is undertaken. Also, all subatomic particles are in
continuous motion, their positions constantly changing.
Physicists use the term "momentum" when referring to this
motion. Momentum is determined by multiplying an object's
velocity by its mass, and it measures the ease with which a
body responds to a force. For example, a butterfly and an
elephant may both be moving at five miles per hour but their
momenta are decidedly different.

Clearly, the constant motion of a subatomic particle on its
own along with the disruptive effects of a measurement attempt make it impossible to determine the particle's position
and momentum at the same time. Neither could be measured
with perfect accuracy. We could establish one with great accuracy but then the other would be that much less accurate.
If we get one or the other of these quantities with 100 percent
accuracy, the other would have an infinite inaccuracy, or uncertainty.

This is the Heisenberg "uncertainty principle," a basic law
of quantum theory, discovered in 1927. According to Werner
Heisenberg, a German physicist, we cannot know with com-

plete accuracy two different quantities, such as location and momentum, simultaneously because the very act of measuring one interferes with the measurement of the other. This principle applies to everyday objects as well as quantum particles, but for larger objects, the effect is so small as to be unnoticeable. For example, we may be able to measure both the location and momentum of a football soaring through the air only to within one part in a billion billionth. But that is certainly close enough to allow a receiver to catch it. It is when we try to measure the same quantities of an electron that the quantum uncertainties dominate. They can be much greater than any measurement we might make. This problem of uncertainty isn't because our instruments aren't good enough. It is simply an impossible task.

Returning to the barrier experiment, we cannot predict which slit an individual electron will go through, nor can we tell exactly where it will land on the detecting screen. But we can know an enormous amount about *all* the electrons that are going through the slits when they are considered as a group. We can determine the probability that an electron, any electron, will be at a given spot at a given time with a given momentum. We don't know which electron it will be, but since all electrons are exactly alike, this is not a vital piece of information. It is enough to know the statistical odds.

Insurance companies use statistical odds all the time. They don't know when any particular individual is going to get sick or which house is going to have a fire or which diamond ring is going to be stolen. But they have compiled many statistics about such events and know the probability of any one of them occurring. Their premium rates are based upon such probabilities. The greater the chance of such events happening, the higher the premiums will be.

Probability is also used in games such as poker or dice.

What is the chance of rolling a seven or of holding a royal flush? There are statistics that have been computed for such odds and experienced players use this information all the time. If we chart the odds of rolling a seven in a game of dice, we would have a curve as shown in Figure 11. As you can see, there is a much greater probability that seven will be thrown because there are more ways for the two dice to add up to seven than any other number. But occasionally the dice do add up to only two or twelve or any number in between.

In other words, the probability of an event taking place can be shown in the form of a curve or a wave that varies in height depending upon its intensity or strength at any given point.

Figure 11. THE ODDS OF ROLLING A SEVEN

There is a greater chance of throwing a seven with a pair of dice than any other number because there are more possible combinations that add up to seven than any other number.

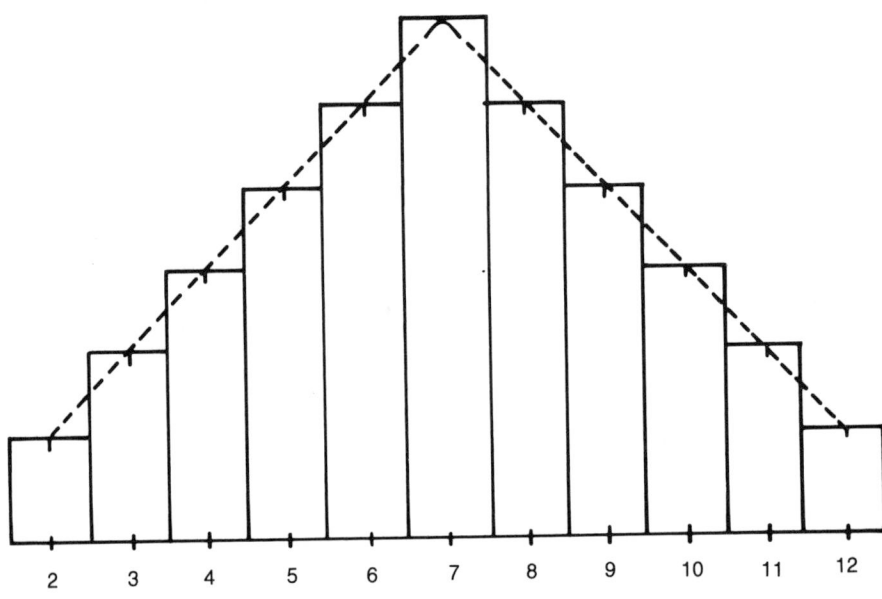

A "probability curve," such as the one in Figure 11, shows the chances of a specific event taking place, such as throwing a particular number on the dice. But it cannot predict the outcome of any specific throw—only the chances.

The intensity curve we produce when studying atomic particles is a probability curve. It tells us the chances of finding an electron at a specific place at a given time. It tells us that a certain number of electrons will jump to a lower energy level and emit photons of a given energy. But it can't tell us whether we will in fact find an electron in the spot we designate or which electron it will be. It can't tell us which electron will jump next or when any specific electron will jump. These individual events occur randomly—there is no order or sequence that they obey.

The concept of probability is not an easy one to accept. Even Albert Einstein is quoted as having said: "God does not play dice." This reluctance to accept quantum uncertainty is understandable. Although Einstein was one of the greatest scientists who ever lived, the idea that naturally occurring events are like a game of chance, that reality is like a dice game, bothered him as much as it bothers most of us. It goes against our common sense and against everything we have been taught. We rely upon a predictable world for our safety and our very existence. And on the macroscopic scale such confidence is usually justified. When we throw a ball, we watch it soar up in the air and then arc downward to our friend some distance away. When we put jelly on our bread, we expect the jelly to spread easily over the bread's surface and to stay there until we eat it. Although the ball sometimes falls short of its mark or the jelly slips off and lands on the floor, these events can be explained by and sometimes blamed upon our own lack of ability.

However, at the atomic level of electrons, protons, and

neutrons, the only predictability is that of probability. This is quantum reality. We cannot see it or feel it without sophisticated instruments. But experiments and theory agree, indicating that it is really "real."

And if further proof is needed, its technological applications should suffice. Here is one example. As you know, the

Figure 12. DISRUPTING THE NORMAL CURVE

Marbles falling through chutes create a normal distribution curve; adding a barrier disrupts this normal curve.

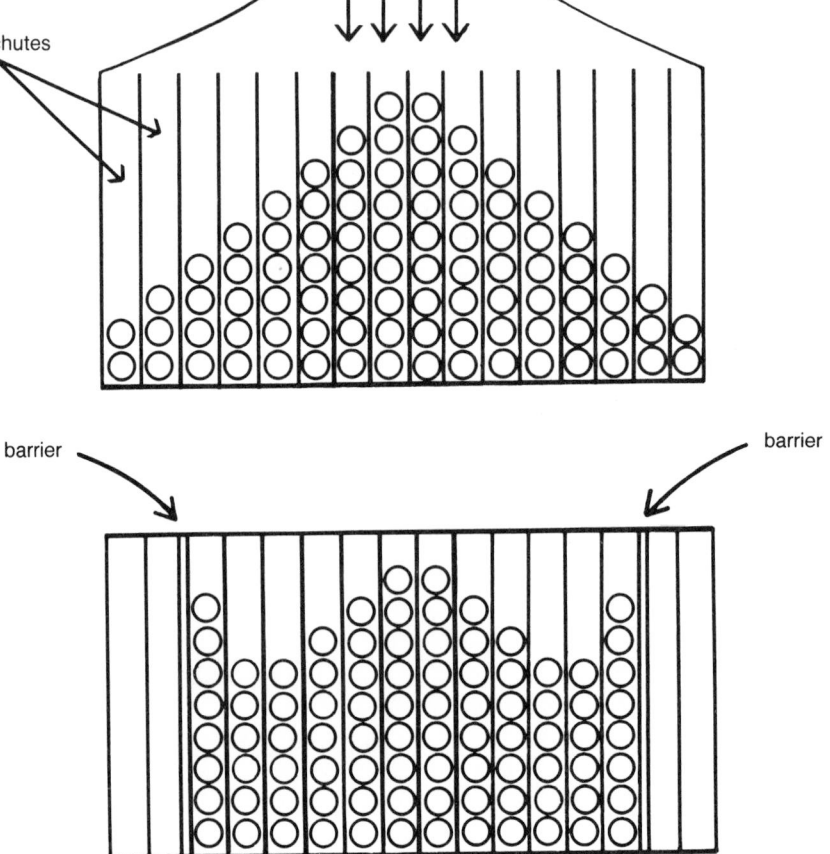

high points on the probability curve indicate the place where most electrons are likely to be found. But a few electrons will also be found at the very lowest points on the curve. What happens if we construct a barrier cutting off the tail ends on either side of the curve? If we were dealing with marbles falling through a chute, those that fall at the very far ends would just pile up against the barrier and spoil the smooth curve, as shown in Figure 12. But electrons and other atomic particles don't behave this way. Somehow a few of them "tunnel" through the supposedly impenetrable barrier and appear on the other side. According to quantum theory, the odds are not only sometimes much lower than what our guess might be, but sometimes they are much higher, as in this example. We might have guessed that the odds of an electron appearing on the other side of a barrier were zero, but this is not so.

Although we cannot visualize what has happened, this tunneling effect has been used by electronic engineers to amplify electronic signals. Transistors and possibly even your digital watch may have components that also use it. It is real. It is quantum reality.

The Rain of Particles

WHILE THE THEORETICAL PHYSICISTS of the 1930s and 1940s were pondering the consequences of Heisenberg's uncertainty principle and probability curves, a new area of research was being explored by experimental physicists. It started in the early 1900s with investigations of electricity detectable in the atmosphere even when there were no electrical thunderstorms present. No one could determine where this penetrating radiation was coming from. Then in 1911, Victor F. Hess, an Austrian physicist, discovered that although this radiation decreased with altitude at first, it started to increase rapidly above about 1.25 miles (2 kilometers). These findings came from manned balloon flights carrying instruments designed to measure such radiation.

Hess's discovery suggested that the radiation was from outer space, and because it was first believed to be a form of electromagnetism, the radiation was called "cosmic rays." Its enormous energy, powerful enough to go through several feet of lead, suggested that it might have a wavelength even shorter than gamma rays. In the 1920s, however, Arthur H. Compton, an American physicist, proved that the earth's magnetic field deflected the cosmic rays, causing more of them to be detected near the north and south magnetic poles. That meant that they could not be electromagnetic radiation, but instead were charged particles. Finally, in the late 1940s, these high-energy particles from outer space were found to be mostly protons, with a small percentage being electrons and heavier nuclei. We now know that these particles have been thrown out into space by stars in various stages of evolution. Some even come from our sun. They travel at nearly the speed of light all through space, and it is this enormous velocity that gives them their high energy.

When these rapidly moving particles from outer space hit the earth's upper atmosphere, they collide with molecules and atoms and break them up. This creates a cascade of smaller bits of matter that rapidly plummet to the ground. Although scientists in the early 1900s did not have the technology to study the original, or primary, cosmic rays from outer space, they were able to devise various kinds of apparatus to detect and identify the resulting secondary particles from the upper atmosphere collisions that were found at the earth's surface.

One of the first instruments for this purpose was the "cloud chamber," which was invented by Charles Wilson, a British physicist, around 1912. Noticing that water vapor will condense on tiny bits of dust to form raindrops, Wilson wondered if such condensation would occur on even smaller objects, such as subatomic particles. Wilson used water vapor in his cloud chambers, but today alcohol is usually used because it evaporates into a vapor more quickly. First, an alcohol vapor cloud is created in a glass enclosure, hence the name "cloud chamber." When a charged particle penetrates the glass and races through the chamber, some of the vapor condenses on the particle to form droplets of alcohol. The trail of condensed drops reveals the particle's path through the vapor. It is seen as a white streak and looks very much like a contrail made by a high-flying jet plane.

In the 1950s Donald A. Glaser, an American physicist,

The fifteen-foot bubble chamber at Fermilab.

developed a similar apparatus called a "bubble chamber." Instead of cool alcohol, it uses liquid hydrogen heated to very near its boiling point. When a charged particle passes through this hot liquid, its energy introduces more heat. The liquid it passes through boils, creating a stream of bubbles that mark the particle's path, just as the condensed drops of alcohol did in the cloud chamber. The trail resembles the stream of bubbles you see rising inside a bottle of soda that has just been opened, although the cause of these bubbles is quite different than those found in a bubble chamber.

A trail of bubbles or droplets through a chamber describes the path a particle has taken. From the number of drops or bubbles created, some idea about the mass and velocity of a particle can also be determined. To learn even more about a particle, scientists placed the north and south poles of a magnet on either side of the chamber. By measuring, among other things, how much and in what direction the particle's path was curved by the magnetic field, they could calculate the particle's momentum and electrical charge. For example, they expected an electron and a proton to curve in opposite directions, but because a proton is so much more massive, they knew that its curve would be entirely different from that of the electron. To use a familiar analogy, when we ride a bicycle, we can "hug" the curb and make a sharp turn at the corner, whereas the driver of a heavily loaded dump truck must make a much wider turn. Otherwise the truck may tip over.

In 1932 Carl D. Anderson, an American physicist, used a cloud chamber with powerful magnets in an attempt to settle the still controversial question of whether cosmic rays were really particles or radiation. He found that the magnets caused the paths of the cosmic rays to be curved, proving they really were electrically charged particles. But Anderson noticed something else happening in the chamber as well. One of the particles made a curving path exactly like an electron but in the opposite direction. That would mean that

Paul A.M. Dirac, center, with Robert Oppenheimer and Abraham Pais, two other world-famous elementary particle physicists, "talking shop" in 1933.

the particle had the same mass as an electron, but with an opposite charge. Anderson had discovered a new particle.

This particle's existence had been predicted in 1930 by the British theoretical physicist Paul A. M. Dirac. From a mathematical analysis of the properties of subatomic particles, including their wave-particle duality, Dirac hypothesized that every subatomic particle should have an "antiparticle," which would be identical in all respects except that it would have the opposite electrical charge. Dirac called these antiparticles "antimatter." Anderson had discovered the antielectron, which was called a "positron" (POSItive elecTRON).

Once the existence of the positron was proven, physicists

found other characteristics of antimatter. When an electron and positron or any other pair of matter and antimatter particles meet each other, it is the end for both of them. They annihilate each other, leaving gamma rays behind. For this reason, there are very few antiparticles in the world as we know it and those that do come into existence are very quickly dispatched. In fact, in the case of the positron, once it meets an electron, the conversion to gamma rays takes only about a millionth of a second. Amazingly, that is long enough to be detected in a cloud chamber.

As short as a millionth of a second may seem, we will be speaking of even shorter time spans later on. A millionth of a second is called a "microsecond." Light, which travels 186,-000 miles per second, can travel 984 feet in one microsecond. That's a little more than the length of three football fields. In a billionth of a second, which is called a "nanosecond," light can travel a little less than a foot (11⅛ inches). The time required for light to move across the diameter of a proton or a neutron is a hundred thousand billion times smaller than a nanosecond. That time period is only 10^{-23} second. This is an important period of time in particle physics and we shall be referring to it later.

Now let's get back to the positrons. Where do they come from? The ones that Anderson detected were created from the energy of the collisions between cosmic rays and upper atmosphere particles. They were part of the secondary radiation that is constantly raining down upon the earth's surface. This is but one example of energy being transformed into matter, which Albert Einstein predicted in his theory of relativity and now-famous equation, $E = mc^2$. This equation states that the mass (m) of an object multiplied by the speed of light squared (c^2) will give us the object's energy equivalence (E).

Einstein showed by his equation that matter and energy are

manifestations of the same thing. Mass is a form of energy. The equation also tells us that a very small amount of mass is equal to an enormous amount of energy because c^2 is a very large number (186,000 times 186,000 miles per second). This has been shown quite dramatically in the development and use of atomic energy in war and peace. It is the underlying principle for all atomic power.

Also, because mass and energy are equivalent, it is possible to describe particles in terms of their energy. In fact, this is one way in which physicists measure them—by their energy content. The basic unit of energy they use is the "electron volt" (eV). This is a very minute amount of energy, much less than the amount expended by a mosquito flapping its wings just once! However, subatomic particles, if they have any mass at all, have the equivalent of much more energy than just one electron volt. For example, the mass of an electron is equivalent to 510,000 eV. Because most particles have energies even greater than that of an electron, physicists use other abbreviations to deal with the higher numbers, as shown in Table 2. The mass of an electron, therefore, is 0.51 MeV; a proton, 938.3 MeV; and a neutron, 939.6 MeV. Note the slight difference between the proton and neutron.

Table 2 ELECTRON VOLT ABBREVIATIONS

Abbreviation	Measurement	Number of eV	
eV	electron volt	1 eV	
KeV	kiloelectron volt	1 thousand (10^3)	eV
MeV	million electron volt	1 million (10^6)	eV
GeV	gigaelectron volt	1 billion (10^9)	eV
TeV	teraelectron volt	1 trillion (10^{12})	eV

Although close, these two particles do not have equal masses and, therefore, do not have equal energies.

We are speaking here of the "rest mass" of each particle. That's how heavy it is when it is motionless relative to the observer. As the particle is accelerated, it gains energy. Because matter and energy are equivalent, a rapidly moving body has a greater mass equivalence than when it is motionless. For example, an electron's rest mass is 0.51 MeV, but it may have a much greater mass equivalence when it is traveling at high velocities.

The positron was not the only new particle discovered while studying cosmic rays with cloud and bubble chambers. Many others were found in the cascade that streamed down from the sky. They had also been created from the energy of the collisions between primary cosmic rays and molecules in the atmosphere, and came down at very high velocities, which gave them a great amount of energy.

First there were the two "mu-mesons," which were discovered by Anderson in 1936 as he continued his investigations of secondary cosmic ray trails. The two mu-mesons were found to have equal masses but opposite charges, one negative and the other positive. They were called mesons because, with a mass two hundred and ten times that of the electron, they were about midway between the lightest and the heaviest particles known at that time. "Meson" means "intermediate one." Their name, mu-meson, was later shortened to "muon." "Mu" is a letter in the Greek alphabet and is written "μ." Therefore, "μ" was adopted as the symbol for the muon.

In 1947 a slightly more massive meson was discovered. It was called the "pi-meson," shortened later to "pion." There are three kinds of pions: negative, positive, and neutral. "Pi" is also a Greek letter and, like the "mu," is used to represent these particles. The symbols for the three pions are: "π^-," "π^+," and "π°." Each is about two hundred and seventy times as massive as the electron. As we will see later, the pions play an extremely important role in particle physics.

Neither muons nor pions exist for very long. They are created and then "decay" in a tiny fraction of a second. ("Decay," in physics, describes what happens to a particle when it breaks up into smaller particles.) The muon, for example, decays into an electron and two neutrinos, which are massless particles that will be described later on. Because of the speed of their decay, muons and pions can only be detected by the tracks they leave when passing through a detection device, such as a bubble or cloud chamber.

The discovery of muons and pions was only the beginning. In 1952 an uncharged particle was found by using the cloud chamber trails left by the particles into which it had decayed. This new particle was called a "lambda" (Λ), again using a letter from the Greek alphabet. Because it had no electrical charge, the lambda left no trail of its own. But as it passed through the cloud chamber, it decayed into a proton and a negative pion. These could be identified by their trails, which started abruptly within the chamber. Using the characteristics of these trails, physicists were able to work backward from the point of the decay and determine the properties of the original particle, the lambda. For example, because it broke up into a proton and a pion, scientists concluded it must have been more massive than a proton.

They also found that the lambda had a much longer lifetime than other particles that were similar to it. This was determined by how long it took to travel through the chamber before it decayed. While the lambda still decayed in a fraction of a second, this fraction was much larger than the lifetimes for other similar particles. Later, new particles were found that also exhibited relatively longer lifetimes. This property was called "strangeness." "Strange" particles take longer to decay than those without this characteristic. It is one of the many features that physicists look for when trying to identify and classify the many bits of matter. Although the term is rather odd, it isn't the only time that physicists have brought a little lightness to an otherwise difficult subject.

To be able to study these subatomic particles in greater depth, it became evident even as early as the 1920s that cosmic ray studies were not sufficient. What were needed were devices that could artificially produce these particles. Then, physicists wouldn't have to wait until something important went through the detectors, just like earlier researchers of electricity had to bide their time until lightning struck. And with devices that could produce enough energy, even more massive particles could be created. For example, Dirac had predicted the existence not only of the positron but also of the antiproton. To produce this particle, whose mass was the same as the proton, required one thousand eight hundred and thirty-six times as much energy as was needed to produce an electron or positron. Such an energy level could be achieved by accelerating particles to high velocities and smashing them into something, just as cosmic rays smash into the earth's atmosphere. Two years before Dirac's prediction, the first of a long series of "accelerators" was developed for this purpose.

7
The Big Machines

THE CONSTRUCTION OF ACCELERATORS began in 1928 with relatively small machines. One of the first was made by two English physicists, John Cockcroft and Ernest Walton. With this early "Cockcroft-Walton generator," protons could be accelerated to energies of almost 400,000 eV. Today, at the Fermi National Accelerator Laboratory (Fermilab) near Chicago, Illinois, a much larger Cockcroft-Walton generator, capable of producing protons with energies of 750,000 eV, is used as the first of four stages in the acceleration of protons.

However, by themselves, such machines are limited to the initial acceleration. To increase the particles' velocities further, other devices were needed. Developed in the early 1930s, these other machines used electrical impulses and powerful magnets that both controlled and accelerated the charged particles to higher energies. As you already know, only charged particles will react to electrical or magnetic forces. Neutrons cannot be used. Therefore, most accelerator experiments use either protons or electrons. The acceleration is done in a series of small pushes, each one elevating the velocity of the particles a little more. The pushes are like those given to a swing, each push causing the swing to go higher.

The first accelerators that used a series of small pushes

The Cockcroft-Walton generator at Cavendish Laboratory, Cambridge, England.

were long straight tunnels called "linear accelerators." At Fermilab, for example, a linear accelerator is used as the second stage in producing high-energy protons. After the protons emerge from the Cockcroft-Walton generator, they are sent down a five-hundred-foot-long tube in which oscillating electrical fields push them along much like a surfer is pushed by a water wave. In this way, the protons are accelerated to energies of 200 MeV.

There are other linear accelerators that are longer and more powerful. One of the largest is the Stanford Linear Accelerator Center (SLAC) at Stanford University in California. Built in the 1960s, it is two miles long and can produce a beam of accelerated electrons equivalent to 30 GeV, the most powerful electron beam in the world. One drawback of linear accelerators, however, is that the energy levels they can achieve by themselves are limited by their length. Because of this, in the 1930s another form of accelerator was also developed.

Ernest Lawrence, an American physicist, built a circular

accelerator that was called a "cyclotron." Less than a foot in diameter, the cyclotron used powerful magnets to keep the accelerating protons on their circular path until they reached an energy level from this motion of about 1.25 MeV. Another model, built in 1931, was only four inches in diameter, but it was capable of producing protons with energies of 80 KeV. By whirling the particles around the track many times so they picked up more and more energy with each revolution, such machines were able to produce particles with far more energy than could be attained with a linear design of a similar size. Lawrence received the Nobel Prize in 1939 for his invention.

As larger cyclotrons were built, particle energies rose. At first there didn't seem to be any limit to such energies. But there was. That limit was determined by the mass of the accelerated particles. Here on earth we measure an object's mass by its weight. For example, a Ping-Pong ball and a golf

Fermilab.

The cyclotron, a circular accelerator, was first developed by the American physicist Ernest Lawrence.

ball are about the same size but their masses and weights are quite different. The golf ball has a greater mass and weight because there are more and heavier molecules of matter in it.

According to Einstein's theory of relativity, as an object is accelerated, its mass increases. This applies to electrons, airplanes, or you and me. In our everyday experience, nothing goes so fast as to become noticeably heavier in weight. Even our fastest jet planes are slow compared to the speed of light, which is the ultimate speed of any material object. It is only when the speed of light is approached that the increase in mass is measurable and becomes a very important consideration in an experiment.

This increase in mass also explains why no material object can be made to go as fast as the speed of light. Its mass would have increased so enormously before it reached this speed that all the energy in the universe would not be enough to accelerate it to any higher speed.

Proof of Einstein's theory came when the cyclotrons accelerated electrons and protons to velocities that were a sizable percentage of the speed of light. The accelerated particles became heavier and heavier as they went faster. As their mass increased, the strength of the magnetic field used to keep them in their circular paths had to be greatly increased.

Eventually, however, the magnetic field, whose strength was fixed in these early models, could not control these massive bodies. The highest energy any cyclotron can produce today is the proton beam of only 22 MeV. That is far better than what the first cyclotrons were capable of, but its use is limited. Such a beam can examine atomic nuclei but its energy is not enough to probe smaller regions. With only a little over 20 MeV, the cyclotron cannot create massive particles like the pion for which 140 MeV is needed, the energy equivalent of the pion mass. Clearly, a new design was necessary, and it came in 1945 when the "synchrotron" was developed.

The synchrotron is also a circular accelerator, but its magnetic field is designed to increase as the particles' velocities increase. In this way, the magnetic strength is "synchronized" with the increasing mass of the electrons or protons, making it possible to reach the desired energy level while still keeping the particles under control. The only limitations upon this design are the size of the ring and the enormous expense involved in building and operating the machine.

The largest proton synchrotron is at Fermilab. (See Figure 13.) Its main ring, which is more than one mile in diameter, is the final stage that protons reach in the acceleration process. Just before that stage, and following their ride down the linear accelerator, they are whirled fifteen times a second around a smaller synchrotron that is five hundred feet in diameter. This raises the protons' energy to 8 GeV, ready for entry into the main ring. Here they are accelerated up to 500 GeV while being guided by a thousand magnets that focus the proton beam within a two-by-five-inch vacuum chamber in the center of the magnets. In one second the protons race around the ring fifty thousand times.

In 1983 Fermilab added a new and more powerful set of magnets to its four-mile-long ring and the synchrotron is now capable of producing acceleration energies up to one trillion electron volts (1 TeV). For this reason, the new ring is called the "Tevatron." It can reach the highest energy level of any accelerator today, but even more powerful and bigger machines are being contemplated for the future. That's quite a growth from the 80 KeV the four-inch cyclotron was capable of producing less than sixty years ago.

With the synchrotron, once the electrons or protons that have been hurled through the machine reach the desired velocity, they are allowed to strike a selected target. This is usually a block of metal or perhaps some liquid hydrogen. The collisions of the high-speed particles into the target's

Figure 13.   FERMILAB

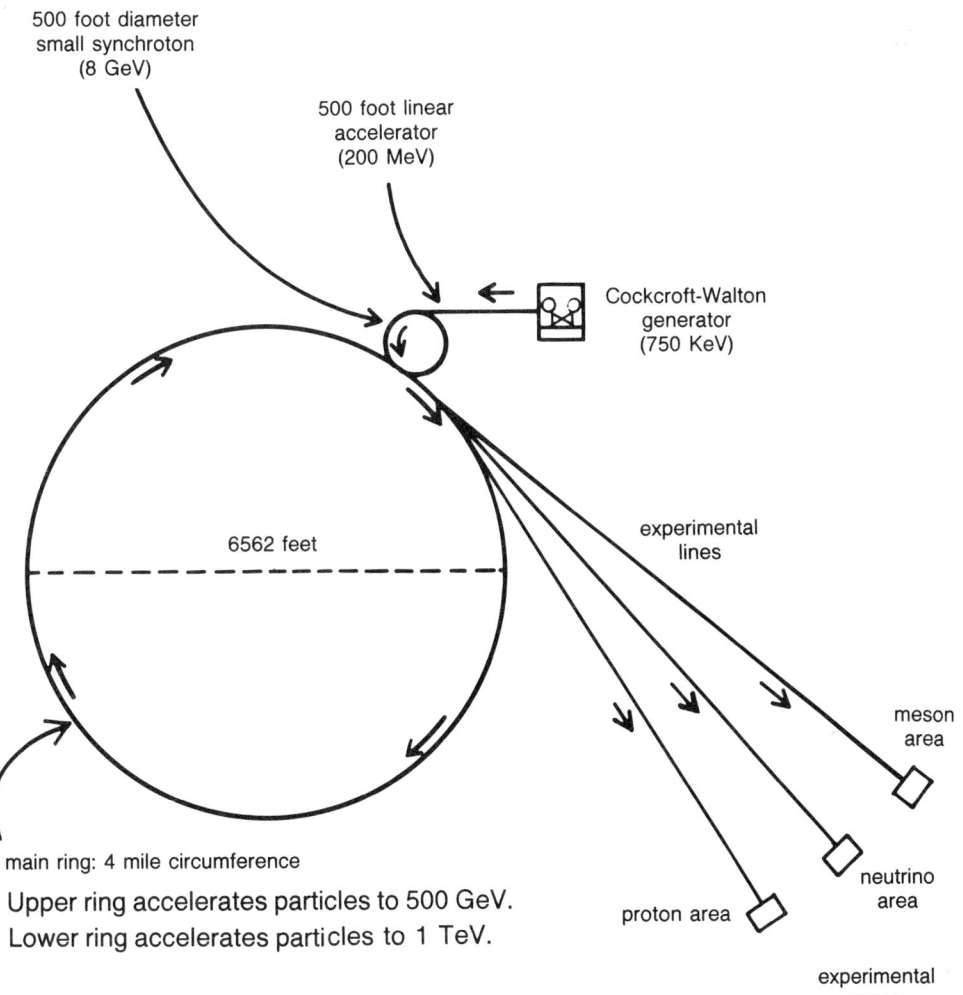

500 foot diameter
small synchroton
(8 GeV)

500 foot linear
accelerator
(200 MeV)

Cockcroft-Walton
generator
(750 KeV)

6562 feet

experimental
lines

meson
area

main ring: 4 mile circumference

Upper ring accelerates particles to 500 GeV.
Lower ring accelerates particles to 1 TeV.

proton area

neutrino
area

experimental
areas

Fermilab.

An aerial view of the Fermi National Accelerator Laboratory, Batavia, Illinois. The largest circle is the main accelerator. Three experimental lines extend at a tangent from the accelerator.

atoms produce all sorts of secondary particles. It is like smashing the eight ball into the closely racked group of balls on a pool table.

Created from the energy of the collision and the breakup of the colliding particles, these secondary particles emerge on the other side of the accelerator's target and spread out from their narrow exit point. The many different kinds of particles that are produced must first be sorted out and identified for further study. Scientists are then able to use magnets and narrow slit openings to direct each type of particle into a separate area. In this way, streams of neutrinos, pions, and other particles have been created and isolated.

Another synchrotron design is called the "electron-positron colliding beam storage ring." As the name suggests, two beams of particles are accelerated in opposite directions and then sent smashing into each other. Not all of the electrons will meet an oncoming positron in such a collision, but those that do create more particles and particles with greater masses than those produced by collisions with stationary targets. In 1973 a colliding beam storage ring was added to the linear accelerator at SLAC. Within two years experiments at this new machine uncovered new particles that proved to be most important in particle physics research. As with most other accelerator laboratories, SLAC is constantly designing larger and more powerful research tools in an effort to produce particles with ever-greater energies.

If it sounds as though these particles are being made out of nothing, this is not so. As you know, matter is a form of energy. A tiny bit of matter contains an enormous amount of energy. To make even the tiniest and least massive particles requires a tremendous input of energy. To create more massive particles, even more energy is needed. Such energy is found in cosmic ray collisions. It is also found in giant accelerators.

Fermilab.

The main tunnel at Fermilab with its two rings of accelerator magnets. The upper ring has operated at an energy of 500 GeV. It is now an injector for the lower ring of superconducting magnets (Tevatron), which can accelerate particles to an energy of 1 Tev.

Many newly made particles do not last very long. In fact, we never see them at all. What we do see are the trails of bubbles and sparks that they leave on photographs taken at the instant of collision. Such trails can also be recorded electronically. Physicists use these trails to identify which bits of matter were there—the particles have signed in even though they are no longer in existence. Since a neutral particle, such as a neutron or a lambda, does not leave a trail, scientists must use the trails of those particles into which it has decayed to determine the properties of the source.

The accelerator is therefore very much like a microscope. But it is designed to "see" bits of matter that are much smaller than anything a microscope could reveal. We use a microscope to magnify objects too small to be seen clearly with the naked eye. An optical microscope uses light rays to illuminate the object being studied. This means that even the most powerful optical microscope cannot clearly "see" ob-

Proton with 300 BeV energy producing twenty-six charged particles in the thirty-inch hydrogen bubble chamber at Fermilab.

Fermilab.

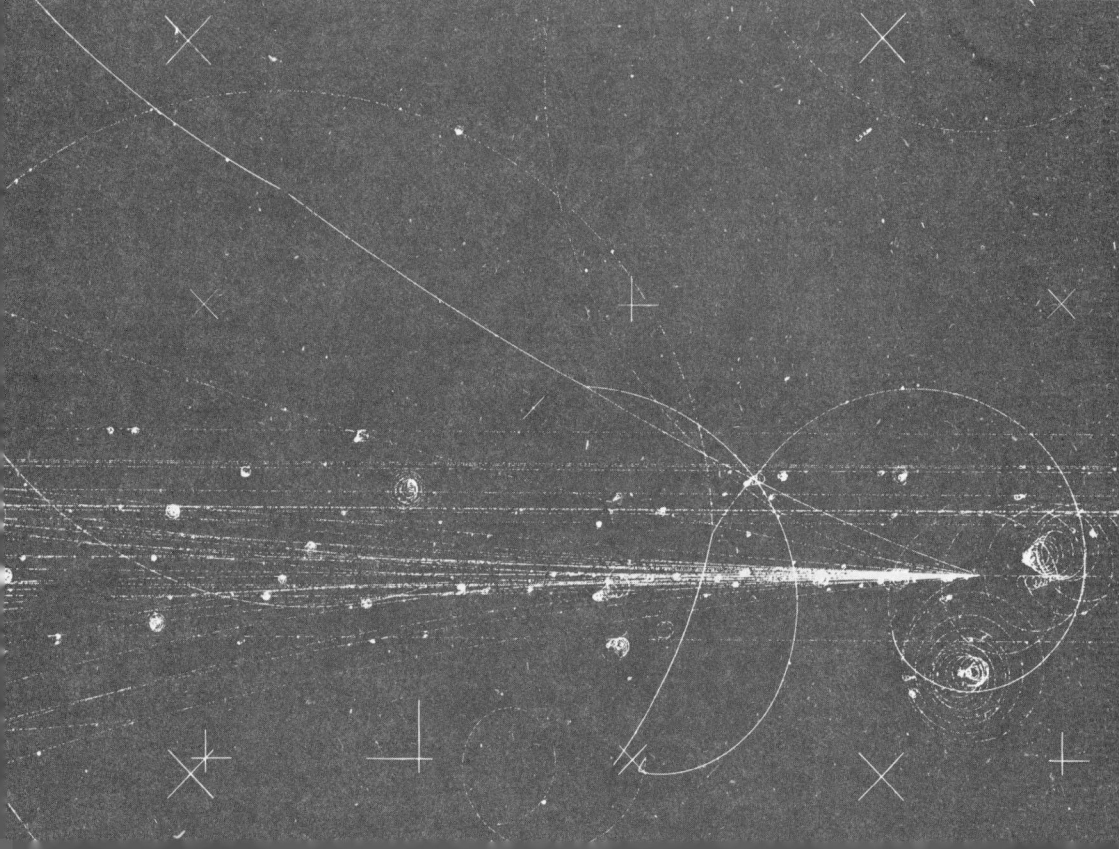

Figure 14. DETECTION OF PARTICLES

If a particle is smaller than a wavelength of visible light, it cannot be seen with an ordinary microscope. The light wave, instead of illuminating it, will pass right by it without detecting it. Therefore, scientists must use wavelengths that are smaller than the particles they wish to "see." High energy electrons and protons have these shorter wavelengths.

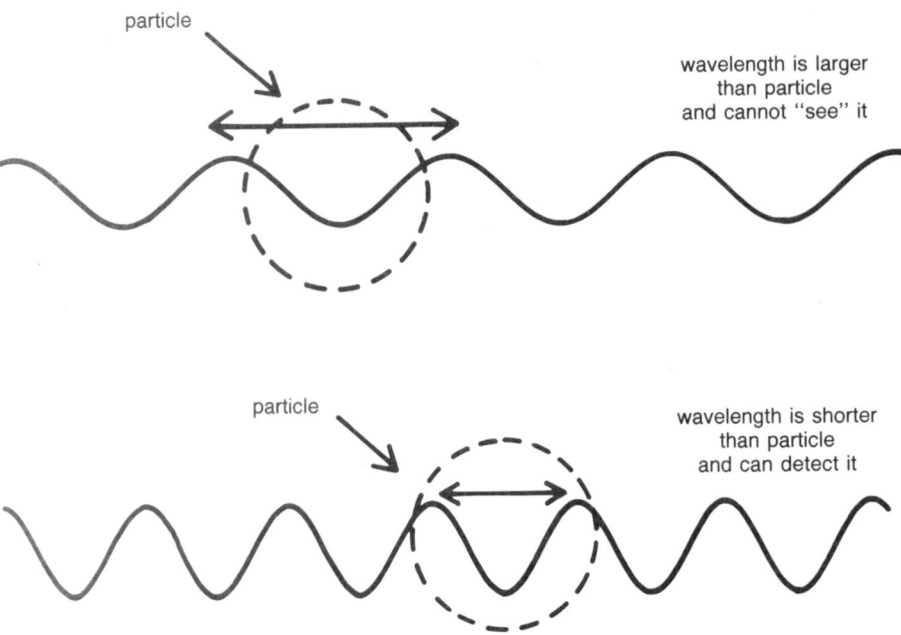

jects that are smaller than the shortest light wave. To make up for this drawback, the electron microscope was developed. It uses electrons, which have wavelengths equivalent to those of X-rays. (X-rays themselves cannot be used because they are too destructive.) Since the electron's wavelength is so much shorter than the wavelength of visible light, the electron microscope can detect objects beyond the scope of optical microscopes. (See Figure 14.) To examine even smaller bits of matter and tinier volumes of space than the electron microscope can reveal, physicists must use particles with yet smaller wavelengths.

Accelerating electrons and protons in cyclotrons and other similar machines to enormous velocities close to the speed of light greatly raises their energies. This shortens their wavelengths, making them as small as those of the most powerful gamma waves. Then, using these accelerated particles as their "needle" probes, physicists can continue their search. The particles that they are now looking for are less than a trillionth the size of a bacterium—which itself is only about one ten-thousandth of an inch! To discover these particles, however, even higher energies may be necessary, which means even larger and more powerful accelerators will be needed. It is ironic that the largest laboratory equipment is needed to explore the tiniest realm of nature.

Decay of the Universe

ACCELERATORS PROBABLY WOULD NEVER have been necessary if the atom had been found to be as simple as many nineteenth-century physicists and chemists believed it to be. In fact, by 1890 some scientists thought that all the important facts about matter and electricity had been discovered. They believed that nothing remained for physicists to do except make more accurate measurements of important quantities whose values were already approximately known.

However, not everyone was satisfied that the atom had been fully explored or that the phenomenon of electricity had been correctly explained. It was still a mystery why spontaneous radiation, or radioactivity, emanated from certain elements. Although Rutherford used this emanation early in the twentieth century to probe the atomic structure, thus discovering the nucleus, neither he nor any of his colleagues knew what it was. Rutherford called the radiation he used in his experiments "alpha rays," to distinguish it from two other kinds of radiation—"beta rays" and "gamma rays"—that also emanated from radioactive substances. All three names came from the first three letters of the Greek alphabet.

Beta rays had been identified as streams of electrons by the French physicist Antoine-Henri Becquerel soon after he discovered radioactivity in 1896. These particles were identical to those that streamed across the cathode ray tube in the experiments described in Chapter Two. Today scientists sometimes refer to an electron as a "beta particle."

Shortly after gamma rays were discovered, they were shown to be radiation similar to X-rays but with shorter wavelengths. As you know, they are found at the very high end of the electromagnetic spectrum and have the greatest amount of energy of any radiation now known.

By 1909 Rutherford, after studying the effects of magnets on alpha rays, confirmed that alpha rays were positively charged particles with four times the mass of the hydrogen atom. This was determined from the direction and amount of deflection caused by magnets as the particles passed through a cloud chamber. They were later identified as the nuclei of helium atoms, which today are often referred to as "alpha particles."

From his experiments, it was evident to Rutherford that radioactivity must be a manifestation of some kind of subatomic change in which particles and energy were shot out from the atom, thus causing its internal structure to be altered. When this happened, the atom became an atom of another element. This change, called a "transmutation of the element," is what the early alchemists had attempted to achieve with lead and copper. However, they were pursuing an impossible goal. In fact, lead is the end product of a whole series of transmutations of radioactive elements.

By 1913, with the development of the Bohr model of the atom, it became clear that although the outer atomic parts were responsible for an element's chemical properties, all radioactivity emanated from the nucleus. Even beta particles came from this tiny remote core. Scientists asked themselves: How is this possible? How can electrons (beta particles), for example, suddenly appear where none were found before? If radioactivity was ever to be understood, they concluded, the atomic nucleus must be explored.

This exploration took place within the first few decades of this century and physicists discovered how the process of transmutation proceeds. As one example, let us consider the scientists' findings about beta particles. While it is true that there are no free electrons in the nucleus of a normal atom, in certain radioactive elements, an unusual phenomenon occurs: The neutrons "decay." One after another they break apart, leaving in their place a proton and an electron.

This phenomenon is unusual because it happens inside the nucleus. When neutrons are single particles outside the atom, such decay is expected and occurs quickly. In a group of free neutrons, for example, about half of them will break up into protons and electrons within about ten and a half minutes. After another ten and a half minutes, half of those remaining will also decay. This breakup continues until all the neutrons are gone.

But neutrons within most atoms do not decay. Such atoms are considered "stable." They do not change. Only in certain radioactive elements do neutrons break up. There, the freed electrons move rapidly away, causing streams of beta rays to emanate from the substance. The breakup itself is called "beta decay."

Once the electron is gone, the atom is left with one more proton and one less neutron than it had before. It therefore has a positive charge until it is able to pick up another electron and become neutral again. Because of the great velocity with which an electron is propelled outward, that electron quickly becomes too far away to be recaptured. However, the atom's positive charge enables it to attract another electron nearby, if one is available, and thus restore the atom's neutral charge. Now the atom has one more proton, one more electron, and one less neutron than it had originally. It has become a different kind of atom; it has been transmuted into a different element.

In the process of beta decay, a very small amount of mass from the nucleus is converted into energy. This gives the freed electron the energy to move away so rapidly. Physicists in the early 1920s were able to measure this energy and the resultant loss of mass. In so doing, they realized that not all the converted mass was accounted for in the electron's energy—some energy was missing. In 1931 Wolfgang Pauli, an Austrian physicist, suggested that perhaps another particle was emitted from the nucleus along with the beta particle. It would be a rather unusual particle, he said, because it would have neither mass nor charge and would move at the speed of light. The idea appealed to the world of physics, and Enrico Fermi of Italy even named this particle "neutrino," which is Italian for "little neutral one." Once the neutron was finally detected in 1932, some physicists, such as Fermi, were even surer that such a particle really existed.

However, the detection of neutrinos is difficult. To be detected, an object, whether it be a subatomic particle or a body of some size, must interact with some other object. This interaction causes a change in the second object that we can observe and measure. Neutrinos are elusive particles because they very rarely interact with anything else. One could pass through the entire earth without having any contact with any other object. They are constantly passing through our bodies without any effect on us or on them. And since the neutrino is neutrally charged, it doesn't even leave a trail in a bubble chamber or on a photographic plate. It is so elusive, in fact, that if we had a lead plate trillions of miles thick, we might stand a chance of detecting one neutrino passing through the plate. Given all this, how could scientists ever hope to find such a particle and prove its existence?

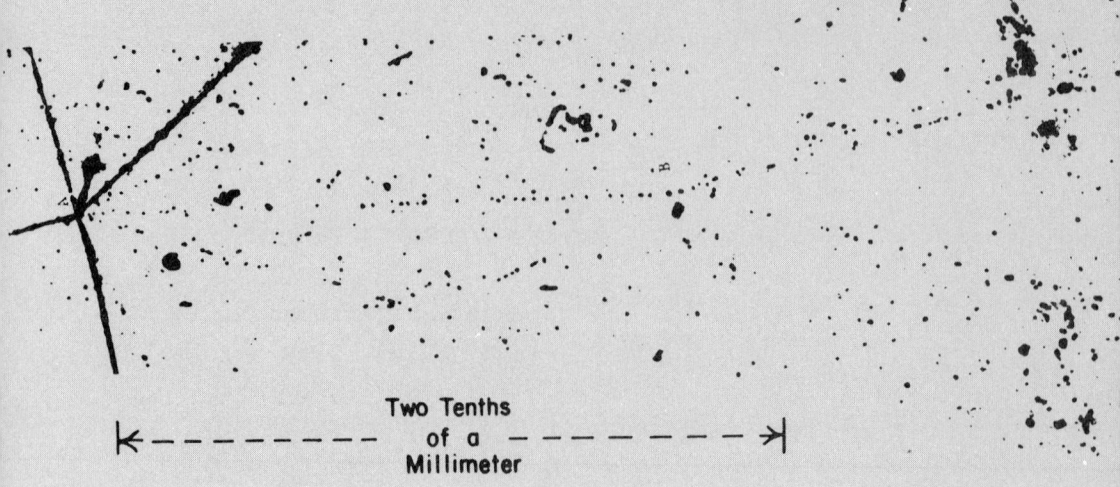

Fermilab.

A neutrino interaction: the black tracks are made by slow moving particles. Fast tracks can be seen in a generally forward direction. One fast track broke up into three other tracks after 0.2 millimeters. This could be the decay of a new particle into three charged particles plus at least one unseen neutral particle.

Various calculations revealed that neutrinos are produced in great numbers in nuclear reactions, such as those that take place in the sun and other stars. With this information, physicists set up an experiment in 1953 near a large nuclear reactor of the Atomic Energy Commission in Georgia. By relying upon the passage of a great many neutrinos, they hoped to considerably increase their chances of detecting even a few. Three years later, and twenty-five years after Pauli's description of it, the first neutrino was found. Since then scientists have learned how to produce streams of neutrinos for further research. As we shall learn later, these energetic particles, used as tiny "needles," have made it possible to probe even smaller parts of the atom. Later we will explore how neutrinos fit into the overall picture.

As for the decay process, physicists have discovered that practically all particles eventually decay even if they are not in radioactive substances. Those in radioactive elements decay in such a way as to be quite noticeable. Others decay so rapidly after they are created that we are often never even aware that they existed in the first place. Of the particles we have discussed so far, only photons, neutrinos, electrons, and possibly protons have been found to be truly stable particles. There are no smaller particles into which these can decay.

Protons are currently suspect as stable particles largely because the latest theories in particle physics predict they are capable of decay. Proof of proton decay would indicate the validity of these theories which, in turn, hold the answer to much that is otherwise unknown about the structure of matter and of the universe.

So far we have no proof of proton decay although extensive experiments using elaborate equipment have been set up in several deep mines throughout the world. Such unusual underground locations have been chosen in order to reduce the possibility of cosmic rays triggering the sensitive instruments. The hundreds of feet of rock above the detectors provide shielding from these energetic particles.

The largest such proton decay detector is two thousand feet below the earth's surface in the Fairpost Salt Mine near Cleveland, Ohio. It is a rectangular tank seventy-eight feet deep and eighty feet across filled with pure water. Water is used because it is relatively inexpensive and easy to handle. And as you know, each water molecule contains two hydrogen atoms, the nucleus of each being a proton. According to current theory, if protons do decay, at least one of the protons in the ten thousand tons of water should decay and be detected approximately every month.

If and when a proton decays, it is expected to become a positron and a neutral pion. (See Figure 15.) The positron very quickly meets an electron and the annihilation of the two produce a photon. The pion also decays rapidly, producing

Figure 15. THE THEORETICAL PROCESS OF PROTON DECAY

The proton (p+) decays into a positron (e+) and a pion (π). The positron meets an electron and the two annihilate each other, leaving a photon. The pion decays into two photons.

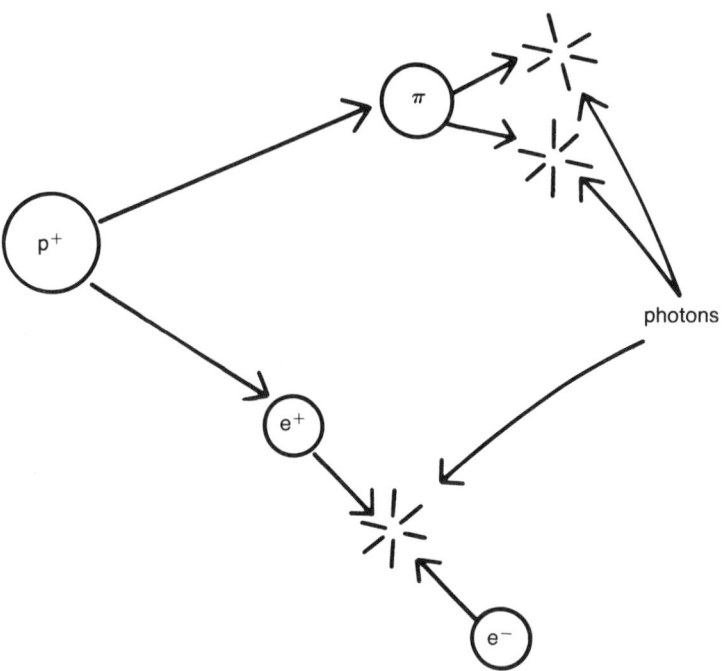

photons

two more photons. Along the walls of the huge proton decay detector are 2,048 photomultiplier tubes. The tubes are able to detect the photons as tiny sparks of electromagnetic radiation. They can also amplify these faint emissions and send the signals to a computer for analysis. A burst of three photons in a certain pattern would be evidence that a proton has decayed.

The experiment at the Fairpost Salt Mine was started in 1982 but so far no positively identified decay event has been reported. This could mean that protons take much longer to decay than has been believed or that the basic theories have to be changed.

Whether or not protons do decay, physicists know for certain that their average lifetime is enormously long. It is estimated that it would take about ten thousand billion billion billion years for even half the protons in the entire universe to decay. It would take another, similar time period for half of those remaining to disappear. If protons do decay, our universe will eventually come to an end. All matter as we know it will decay into electrons, positrons, photons, and neutrinos and will be incapable of chemically binding together again. This may be the ultimate end, but it will be many billions of years before anything so drastic occurs. Let us turn our attention now to the question of what holds the universe we have now together. What are the forces in nature that make the world around us the way it is? Later we will consider proton decay again when we look more closely at current theories of particle physics.

The Sticky Bosons

SCIENTISTS AND PHILOSOPHERS have speculated for centuries about the force that keeps us from flying off the earth into space. It was Sir Isaac Newton in the middle of the seventeenth century who recognized that this same force is also responsible for keeping the planets in their orbits and for causing objects to fall to the ground. This is, of course, the gravitational force with which we are all familiar.

When physicists began to investigate electricity and magnetism, they discovered another force, electromagnetism, which was found to be much stronger than gravitation. A small magnet, for example, will pull a bunch of paper clips up from the table and keep them from falling down again. Static electricity will also cause certain materials to cling to each other, overcoming any gravitational pull. Electrically charged particles with the same sign, whether positive or negative, repel each other while those with opposite signs are attracted to each other.

Electromagnetism's attractive and repulsive force explained how the atom's electrons are held in place—they are attracted to the positively charged protons in the nucleus. But the discovery of the nucleus at the beginning of the twentieth century raised another question for physicists: What held the nucleus together? The protons in the nucleus are all positively charged and are much closer to each other than any electron. Therefore, according to the fundamental laws of electricity, they should repel each other, making the formation of a nucleus impossible. Because this obviously doesn't happen, physicists reasoned that there must be another force, one that is stronger than electromagnetism. Called the "strong nuclear force," it was later found to be about a hundred thirty times more powerful than electromagnetism.

The scientists found that unlike the gravitational and electromagnetic forces, the strong nuclear force is felt only over very tiny distances. For example, the protons in an average nucleus are only about 10^{-13} centimeter apart. At that distance the strong force is very effective and is able to overcome the electromagnetic force, keeping the protons close together within the nucleus. But if the protons are separated by a distance greater than approximately their own diameters, the strong force has no such effect.

There is also a fourth force which, instead of holding systems together, causes the slow and relatively rare decay of particles into smaller, more stable bits of matter, such as protons, electrons, photons, and neutrinos. When the theory

Table 3 THE FOUR FORCES

Name	Strength Compared to Strong Force	Effective Range	What It Does
Gravitation	6×10^{-39}	Infinite	Holds massive objects together; gravity
Electromagnetism	1/137	Infinite	Holds atom together; binds electron to nucleus
Strong	1	10^{-13}cm	Holds atomic nucleus together
Weak	10^{-5}	10^{-15}cm	Causes decay of particles

for it was worked out in 1934 by Enrico Fermi, this force was called the "weak force," because it is not as powerful as either the strong or electromagnetic forces. The radioactivity found in certain elements is a product of this force, as is the decay of many of the particles created by the giant accelerators and by cosmic rays. Like the strong nuclear force, the effect of the weak force is extremely short-range. However, without its ability to get rid of all kinds of unusual particles that are constantly being created by the rain of cosmic rays upon our atmosphere, the world we are accustomed to might be a very different place than it is now.

Although we are most familiar with the gravitational force and it is certainly the most far-reaching of all the forces, extending to the very end of the universe, it is the weakest when one considers interactions between individual quantum particles rather than between particles in bulk. An electron and proton, for example, are attracted by the electromagnetic force some billion billion billion (10^{27}) times more than they are by the gravitational one. This is because the effect of gravitational attraction depends upon large concentrations of mass, which usually are neutrally charged. Then the combined gravitational effect of all the particles in a body controls each individual particle within it, thus holding the body together. However, when studying individual particles, this force is not important compared to the others and can usually be ignored.

Just what causes the four forces that control the way matter and energy exist and evolve in the universe? In 1932 Werner Heisenberg, who discovered the uncertainty principle, presented a hypothesis to explain the strong nuclear force. This concept has since been successfully applied to the others as well. Heisenberg suggested that protons are held together in the atomic nucleus by constantly exchanging a special kind of particle with the atom's neutrons. This exchange causes the protons to change into neutrons and vice versa in very rapid succession. So rapid, in fact, that before the proton can be repelled by a neighboring proton, it receives an exchange particle from a neutron, which reverses the identity of both of them. And before the newly created proton can be repelled, it switches back to being a neutron by the same process. According to this hypothesis, at any instant the atom has the required number of protons and neutrons in its nucleus, but they keep changing back and forth. The time required for such exchanges is smaller than any time span we can imagine, as tiny as about a trillionth of a trillionth of a second.

To help understand this exchange phenomenon, let us compare it to a commonplace event—a game of catch. We can see the ball that the two players throw back and forth, and we quickly recognize that it is the ball and the game that are keeping them together. Without the ball they would go off to do something else, possibly separating from each other.

Now imagine that an alien being from outer space suddenly lands near the two players. He can see them moving about but he cannot see the ball. It goes back and forth too quickly for his poor eyesight to detect it. He watches, puzzled, because he cannot understand what keeps the humans together. He decides finally that some mysterious "force" holds them bound to each other so that they cannot wander away. He never suspects that some unseen, undetectable object is actually responsible.

According to Heisenberg's hypothesis, when physicists first started studying atomic particles, they were, in a sense, like the visitor from outer space. There did seem to be a "force" holding the electrons to the atomic nucleus. And another "force" seemed to hold the particles in the nucleus together. Scientists reached these conclusions because they could not see the "balls" that these particles were "throwing" back and forth. Their "eyesight" was not good enough.

When the cause of the forces was understood to be an interaction between particles (the "players") in the form of an exchange of special types of particles (the "balls"), scientists started referring to the four forces as "interactions." They then went looking for the exchange particles. Collectively, these special particles are referred to as "gauge bosons," although sometimes other particles can be exchanged. For example, it turned out that Heisenberg's exchange particle was not a gauge boson.

The name "boson" honors Satyendra Bose, an Indian physicist who did much work in this field. There are many kinds of bosons; the term "gauge" is used for one specific type—those involved in particle exchanges. They are the glue that holds all else together and their strength, their "stickiness," is a measure of the strength of the interactions.

One of these gauge bosons, the photon, is familiar to you from previous chapters. In the 1920s Heisenberg, Pauli, and Dirac started working on a theory that described the photon as the electromagnetic interaction's gauge boson. At that time only five subatomic particles were known—the electron, proton, neutron, photon, and neutrino—and not all of these had actually been detected yet. However, scientists recognized that the subatomic realm was very different from the macroscopic world and that a new theoretical framework was necessary to describe it. The "classical mechanics" of Newton and others who followed him had described the behavior and motion of macroscopic objects; now with the Heisenberg, Pauli, and Dirac theory "quantum mechanics" was used to describe the physics of the atom.

Their theory, called the "quantum electrodynamics theory" (QED), was not completed until after World War II. It has not only been proven correct but it is now considered to be the most precise theory ever presented in physics. QED was the first "relativistic quantum field theory," incorporating Einstein's special theory of relativity with quantum mechanics. Its success encouraged physicists to develop other relativistic quantum field theories, using QED as a model. Some have been exceptionally successful in predicting the properties of the other gauge bosons and the corresponding interactions. These gauge bosons will be described in later chapters. We'll begin with a closer look at the photon.

10

"Cinderella" Particles

WHERE DO GAUGE BOSONS come from? Why can't physicists see them when they're being exchanged? And if they can't be seen, how do we know these exchanges are occurring? To understand how modern physicists explain these phenomena, we must go back to the uncertainty principle. You remember that it is impossible to know exactly what both the momentum and the position of a particle are at the same time. If we know one precisely, the other will be completely unknown, making our information quite useless.

Momentum and position are not the only pair of variables that are affected by the uncertainty principle. Another such pair is the energy of a particle and the time it takes to measure that energy.

How do we measure the energy of anything? For exact measurements, we must use an energy-measuring device, a probe. Consider heat and light which are, as you know, forms of energy. A thermometer put into a hot oven, for example, measures the temperature inside. The photometer on a camera measures the amount of light available to take a picture. Each of these measuring devices requires a certain amount of time to register. It takes time for the mercury in the thermometer or the needle on the photometer to move to the correct position. Until that happens, there is no way to know the amount of heat or light energy that is present.

Let us say that it takes ten seconds for the thermometer to measure the oven's temperature. If that is so, it is impossible to know what the temperature of the oven is after only five seconds, for instance, or eight seconds. The final measurement only gives us the overall energy (heat in this case) for the time period of ten seconds. What if the oven heat fluctuates during this time? Then we have no way of knowing if it did or by how much. In other words, the longer it takes to make an energy measurement, the less accurate we can be about the amount of energy at any given moment. To be more certain about any fluctuations, the time period must be shortened.

What would happen if we used a faster thermometer? That would reduce the time it takes for the probe to work, but even the quickest requires some time to register, even if it's only a split second. The measurement can never be instantaneous because a zero time period does not allow any interaction to take place. To detect anything, energy or matter, some interaction is necessary. Otherwise there is nothing to measure.

None of this may be very important in the kitchen, but when we enter the quantum world, such uncertainty takes on much more meaning. As with the oven, a certain amount of time is always needed to measure the energy of a particle. It cannot happen instantaneously. It may take only a tiny fraction of a second, but even in that time period the energy may fluctuate. We have no way of knowing if it did or by how much.

According to quantum mechanics, the energy does fluctuate within time periods too short to ever be measured, and the shorter the period is, the greater the energy fluctuation can be. When increases in energy occur, they do not always stay as energy. Instead they may become new particles, which come into existence and are converted back into energy once again, all within the time period of the fluctuation. Because more massive particles require more energy to come into existence, they can only do so when the time period is extremely short and more energy is available. And because they are converted back to energy much faster, their lifetimes are much shorter than less massive particles. Usually only electrons and positrons make an appearance since they have very little mass and therefore require relatively small amounts of energy. Theoretically, however, any kind of particle, no matter how massive, can be created naturally as long as the necessary energy is available. These creations and annihilations are occurring all through the universe, even in the empty vacuum of space. Because more massive particles require more energy to come into being and live a much shorter period of time, there are far fewer of them at any instant than there are of lighter varieties. But all are created and all are quickly annihilated to become part of the energy content of the vacuum once again.

If this goes against all your commonsense reasoning, remember that we are talking about a substratum of matter where such reasoning must be cast aside. As you recall from Chapter Six, Einstein showed in $E=mc^2$ that matter (or mass) is a form of energy. One can be changed into the other. A very small amount of mass is the equivalent of a tremendous amount of energy. Scientists have been able to convert energy to mass in the giant accelerators and mass to energy in atomic power plants. The fact that nature is able to and does make the same conversions all the time should come as no surprise.

These transient bits of matter and antimatter are called "virtual particles" to distinguish them from "real" particles. We can't detect them although their properties can be calculated, and they do have an effect on the "real" particles around them. For example, except for the extremely small electrons, the space in the atom outside the atomic nucleus is basically empty—a vacuum. But in it is an electromagnetic field that holds the electrons to the nucleus. The energy in this field fluctuates rapidly. We cannot measure these changes because they are too short-lived, but the excess energy is constantly being used to create pairs of virtual particles—mainly electrons and positrons. These particles are created and annihilated in rapid order, producing energetic photons when they disappear. They cannot be detected, but the effects of these photons on the energy of the orbiting electrons can be measured.

As you know, this interaction between photons and electrons was predicted by the QED theory, and experiments and mathematical analysis have proven its occurrence. Photons are the "balls" that are thrown between protons and electrons. They are the "force" that holds these "real" particles together in the atom; they are the gauge bosons for the electromagnetic interaction.

Existing particles, such as protons and neutrons, can also emit and absorb virtual ones. Like a quick "loan" from a bank, a proton, for example, may "borrow" energy from an increased amount around it and "fluctuate" into itself and a virtual particle. It then returns the "loan" before anyone knows about it and becomes just one particle again. Once again, the shorter the fluctuation, the more massive the new virtual particle can be and the shorter its lifetime will be.

After it has been emitted, a virtual particle does not sit still. However, a virtual proton is too massive and short-lived to move more than its own diameter. It is reabsorbed by the original proton, which then returns the "loaned" energy to its surroundings. As long as the virtual Cinderella gets back before the clock strikes twelve, all is well and no one is the wiser.

To create a virtual proton requires the energy equivalent of a proton's mass. This can only be accomplished if the fluctuation is of very short duration, about 4.3×10^{-24} second. If the fluctuation is longer than this, less energy is available for the loan, and the original proton can only produce a virtual particle that is less massive than itself. Because this smaller creation is lighter, it can travel farther, perhaps several times the distance of the proton's diameter.

If another proton or a neutron happens to be close by, as they are in an atomic nucleus, the virtual particle may be absorbed by that proton or neutron instead of returning to its original base. As the virtual particle travels between these two nuclear particles, which are referred to as "nucleons," each is very slightly attracted toward it. This motion, which can be detected, can be compared to the motions of the ball players getting ready to throw or catch. Scientists studying the nucleons' motions couldn't "see" the virtual particle itself and, therefore, like our fictitious alien visitor, concluded that the nucleons were held together by a strong force, stronger than the electromagnetic one. Before Heisenberg's hypothesis about this phenomenon in 1935, they could not explain it any other way.

Heisenberg turned scientific thinking away from the "force" concept to that of an "interaction" between particles. According to his ideas, exchange particles mediated these interactions. If Heisenberg's hypothesis was to be proven correct, these intermediary particles had to be found and identified. The first step in this process was to calculate the properties each would have. Then would come the search for the particles themselves.

In the mid-1930s the Japanese physicist Hideki Yukawa

presented a mathematical analysis of the strong interaction, using Heisenberg's concept of intermediary particles. These virtual particles, he said, would be exchanged in strong nuclear interactions. Yukawa modeled his theory after QED, which was then well along in its development. According to his calculations, such virtual particles would be two to three hundred times as massive as electrons, but much less massive than protons. Because their mass lay between that of electrons and protons, Yukawa called these particles "mesons," which, as you recall, means "intermediate ones." He showed that with such a mass, they would be able to travel the distance between the protons and neutrons in the nucleus.

There was no particle known in 1934 that had such a mass. Three years later, however, the muon, described in Chapter Six, was discovered. Although it was at first thought to be Yukawa's predicted particle, scientists soon learned that the muon did not respond to the strong interaction. Clearly, it could not be the sought-after meson.

It wasn't until 1947 that Yukawa's meson was finally detected. At that time a group of English physicists were studying the results of cosmic ray collisions with our atmosphere. They found tracks of muons but also saw those of somewhat heavier particles, another kind of meson. The tracks of these mesons indicated that, unlike the muons, they interacted strongly with nucleons when they came close to them. Therefore, the scientists concluded that these particles must be what Yukawa predicted. These were the "pi-mesons," or "pions," that were described in Chapter Six. The pion is the strong nuclear interaction's intermediary particle. However, it is not a gauge boson. Later we will learn about the strong interaction's boson and find out how the pion fits into the particle picture.

Each of the other interactions also has its associated gauge

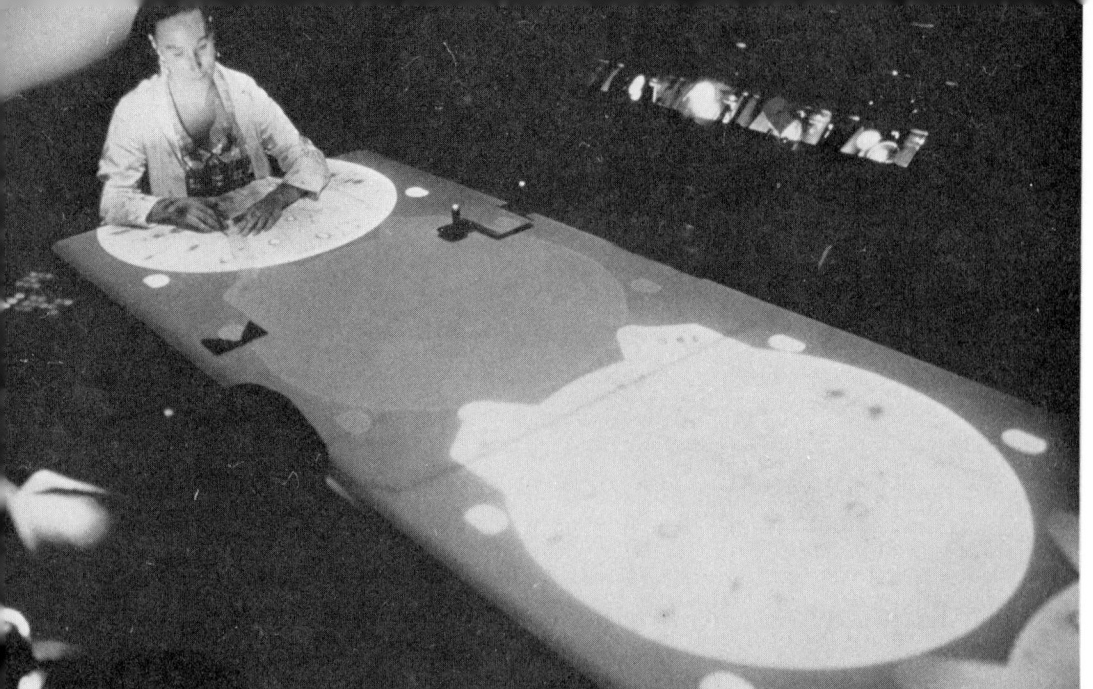

Fermilab.

A researcher studies photographs of particle trails that were recorded in the bubble chamber at CERN. Three different views taken of a single event are projected for measurement. Millions of such photographs must be analyzed for a single experiment.

bosons, which theoretically are exchanged between the particles that respond to their particular interaction. The gravitational force boson has been called the "graviton," although it has not been detected or created in any artificial manner. The expectation is that such a discovery will eventually be made. In 1982 and 1983 the weak interaction bosons were detected at the European Center for Nuclear Research (CERN) in Geneva, Switzerland. These are called the "intermediate vector bosons" and are designated by the symbols: "W^+," "W^-," and "Z°." Carlo Rubbia of Italy and Simon van der Meer of the Netherlands were awarded the Nobel Prize in 1984 for their contributions to this research.

We have seen how a particle exchange between two charged particles, such as protons and electrons, produces the electromagnetic interaction. This exchange takes the

Figure 16. FEYNMAN DIAGRAM SHOWING THE ELECTROMAGNETIC INTERACTION

Richard Feynman, an American theoretical physicist, showed how the different interactions could be calculated with the aid of diagrams such as this one, which represents a very complicated mathematical expression in a simplified form.

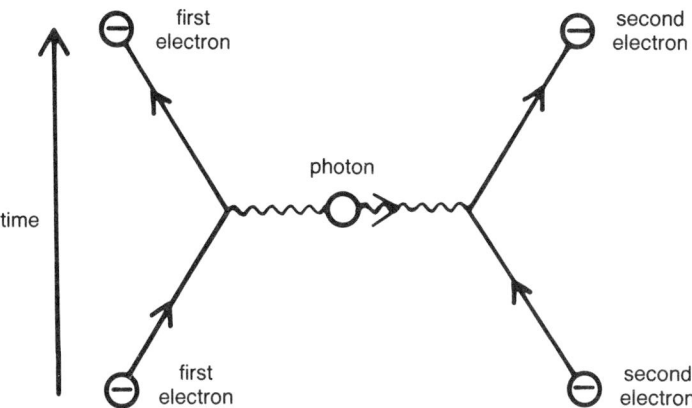

form of photons. (See Figure 16.) In a similar manner, the weak exchange takes the form of W- or Z-particles. (See Figure 17.) This exchange causes weak interactions, such as

Figure 17. FEYNMAN DIAGRAM ILLUSTRATING A WEAK INTERACTION

What appears to be a force is actually an intermediary particle crossing the space between two other particles, thus enabling them to feel each other's presence and react to it.

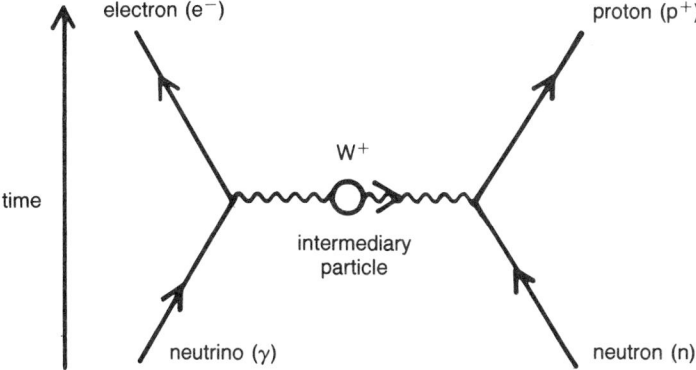

the beta decay of neutrons. However, W- and Z-particles, unlike photons, are very massive, about 80–100 GeV. It is no wonder, then, that early accelerators could not produce any of these particles for physicists to study. Because they are so massive, the intermediate vector bosons require enormous amounts of energy to come into existence, and until recently man-made accelerators didn't have such energy capabilities. But nature has and does. Vector bosons and other virtual particles are continually being created. Either they are absorbed by other particles or they are converted back into energy. None may last very long, but more are being created to take their place.

The space between the stars and galaxies that we usually think of as empty is seething with energy and virtual particles. The universe is a much stranger place than most people had ever imagined. The quantum world is ever present.

11
Hadrons and Leptons

SCIENTISTS KNOW of the existence of virtual particles only by the effects they have on other particles. These other particles may also have very brief lifetimes because of their instability, but they are not virtual—they have not been created by energy fluctuations. Unstable particles can be created, for example, by cosmic ray collisions or by collisions of atomic particles in accelerators.

Thus, there are virtual muons and pions as well as the unstable ones found in cosmic ray debris. The difference between them lies in the manner in which they come into being. We know that electrons are stable particles and are believed to live forever, but virtual electrons have very brief existences.

Stable, unstable, and virtual particles all competed for the attention of particle physics researchers, and by the 1950s physicists knew there were far more particles than they had bargained for—and they kept finding more. For example, after the pion was discovered in 1948, more powerful cyclotrons were built that enabled scientists to produce and experiment with streams of pions in their laboratories. At that time nucleons and pions were the only particles known that responded to the strong interaction. As a group, they were all called "hadrons" from the Greek word for "strong." From the pion experiments, scientists hoped to learn how hadrons interacted with each other and thus find out more about the strong interaction. Instead they discovered an entirely new state of matter—the "nucleon resonance."

In the experiment that produced these resonances, a beam of pions was aimed at a target of protons. Most of the pions went right past the target and did not interact with any of the protons—their paths were not changed in any way. But a few pions did interact—their paths were altered away from the original stream. In these cases, the pion's energy, when combined with the proton's energy (or mass equivalence), fell within narrow energy limits of the energy of a nucleon resonance. The unaffected pions did not have this specific energy.

In the 1940s and early 1950s, when these pion experiments were conducted, the interaction between protons and pions was called a nucleon resonance because the proton (the nucleon) was considered to be transformed, or to resonate, very briefly into a new particle with a much greater energy. Further experimentation showed that the neutron-pion interaction produced similar results. The two original particles, the nucleon and pion, swiftly fused together to create a new particle called a "delta." Its symbol is: "Δ." If the pion is positively charged, the delta is written "Δ^{++}" to show that the delta has two positive charges. Figure 18 illustrates the way such an interaction is represented. The double line connecting the two circles shows that it is a resonance.

Scientists found that the lifetime of a delta is about 4×10^{-23} second, which is approximately the amount of time it takes for light to cross an atomic nucleus. Longer lived particles, by comparison, exist long enough to leave trails of several inches in a bubble chamber or on a photographic plate. Because delta particles live so short a time, they leave no such trails and can only be detected by pion-nucleon interactions. However, as short as this may be, the delta lifetime is longer

Figure 18. FEYNMAN DIAGRAM SHOWING RESONANCE

A proton (p+) and a positively charged pion (π+) interact with each other briefly forming a delta (Δ++).

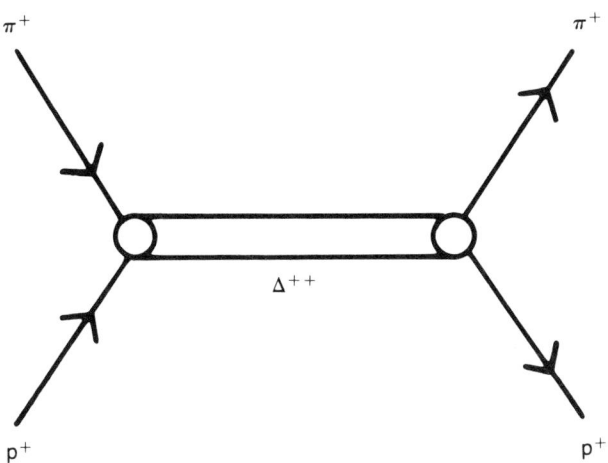

than the time required for a strong interaction to occur. The exchange of virtual particles between nucleons takes only 10^{-24} second!

Besides the Δ^{++}, three other kinds of deltas have been discovered, each with its own charge. (The charge is determined by what kind of pion-nucleon interaction takes place.) Their symbols are: "Δ^+," "Δ°," and "Δ^-." The delta energy, which is a combination of the pion and nucleon energies, is about 1,236 MeV. Therefore, although the delta may exist only for a split fraction of a second, it is far from tiny compared to an electron, photon, or neutrino.

Finding the delta was one of the first indications that there were many more hadrons than the few already known. In fact in the early 1950s the more powerful accelerators began to produce many hadrons that exhibited the strange property. You will remember that these hadrons have relatively longer lives than other particles and therefore leave detectable trails in cloud chambers.

Among the hadrons that were found were the "sigma" (Σ) particle, discovered in 1953, and the two "xi" (Ξ) particles, discovered in 1954. All of these strange particles live 10^{-10} second, which is a much longer lifetime than the delta's.

Physicists reasoned that if delta particles are formed by pion and nucleon interactions, other hadrons could also create such resonance particles. By 1961 another resonance had been produced, this time with a lambda-pion interaction. Thus began a flood of new particles. In the 1960s practically every issue of a scientific journal proclaimed the discovery of yet another particle, each with its own name or number. The list was at times referred to as the hadron "zoo." Physicists now believe that there are an infinite number of hadrons that can be created if the right amount of energy is available. Most of these are extremely unstable and decay rapidly into more stable particles.

The proton and neutron are the best known hadrons of the hundreds that have been discovered. They are also the most stable. However, even in the 1960s scientists knew that none of the hadrons were the sought-after elementary particles. First of all, there were too many of them and none exhibited the characteristics of a pointlike object. The proton was already known to have a specific volume, and the other newly discovered hadrons were also believed to take up space. In fact, many theories of the 1960s treated hadrons as tiny spheres rather than as pointlike objects even though they did not appear to have any internal structure. It was also known that hadrons had an electric charge and magnetic properties and that they could spin around like tops—or at least that's how the "spin" property was usually described.

A word of caution is necessary here. Although we can describe hadrons as spherical bodies spinning around like the earth and moon, that really isn't a true picture. Subatomic particles cannot be depicted that way and when we attempt to do so we lose touch with quantum reality. Physicists can describe the spin of a quantum particle mathematically but they are not treating it as they would the rotation of the earth or the sun or a soccer ball.

However, the spin property gave scientists a way to start classifying hadrons because, like other quantum properties such as electric charge and strangeness, spin is quantized. Only certain spin values are permissible. In this way, it is similar to the specific energy jumps that electrons are permitted in an atom. Spins must be in integer (1, 2, 3 . . .) or half-integer ($\frac{1}{2}$, $\frac{3}{2}$, $\frac{5}{2}$ . . .) units. Hadrons with integer spins are called "mesons"; those with half-integer spins are "baryons." This distinction is important because baryons and mesons behave very differently in strong interactions. The proton and neutron are baryons with spin $\frac{1}{2}$. The pion is a meson with spin 0; it does not rotate at all.

You remember that "meson" originally referred to those particles, such as the muon and pion, with masses midway between the electron and proton. This definition is no longer used. Scientists have since discovered that some mesons are more massive than a proton, and a muon is not even a hadron! Like the electron and neutrino, the muon does not respond to the strong interaction and is therefore not part of the hadron zoo.

Then where does the muon belong? Along with the electron and neutrinos and a few other particles that will be described shortly, the muon is involved in electromagnetic interactions and in the weak interactions that control radioactive decay. All of these particles are called "leptons," which comes from the Greek word for "small." Like hadrons, leptons all have specific spin values, in this case ½.

However, there is an even more fundamental distinction between all these particles. This classification was actually hypothesized by Enrico Fermi as early as 1926 and was later proven to be a basic division of particles by W. Pauli in 1940. Like the meson-baryon classification of the hadrons, this distinction is based upon the spin property but it includes all particles—hadrons, leptons, and gauge bosons. Those particles that have spins of half-integer values (½, ³⁄₂, ⁵⁄₂, and so on) are called "fermions." The name honors Enrico Fermi whose research in nuclear physics earned him the Nobel Prize in 1938. The fermion category includes leptons as well as all the hadrons that are baryons. For example, protons, neutrons, electrons, and neutrinos are all fermions.

Particles that have spin values of zero or whole integers (1, 2, 3, and so on) are called "bosons" and, of course, this includes the gauge bosons. Hadrons that are mesons, such as the pion, for example, are also bosons because they, too, have whole-integer spins. The boson-fermion grouping of particles is such an important classification system because, unlike any other system, no interaction has yet been found that might possibly convert one category into the other. As more theoretical and experimental work is done, however, scientists may discover such an interaction. We will learn more about this in later chapters.

Table 4 shows the fermion-boson classification system and gives some examples of each type of particle. Because the known leptons are so few in number, they can all be listed: the electron, muon, and tau, their associated three neutrinos, and the corresponding six antiparticles. The leptons are all considered elementary particles because, by present experimental data, they are pointlike with no internal structure.

The electron, of course, is the most well-known lepton. It has the smallest mass of any charged particle.

The muon is two hundred times more massive than the electron. For this reason, it has been called a "fat electron." Nevertheless, the muon is also a structureless particle and is considered elementary in nature. It does decay into smaller particles, one of which is the electron. When the muon was first discovered in 1937 among the debris of particles created by cosmic rays, physicists at first believed it to be the mediating particle of the strong interaction. When they found it did not respond to this force, they were puzzled. Only when the distinction between leptons and hadrons was made did they know how to classify this particle.

Table 4 CLASSIFICATION OF SUBATOMIC PARTICLES

FERMIONS (half-interger spin values)		BOSONS (integer spin values)	
Baryons (Hadrons)	Leptons	Mesons (Hadrons)	Gauge Bosons
Proton (p)	Electron (e)	Pion (π)	Photon
Neutron (n)	Muon (μ)	Kaon (k)	Gluon
Sigma (Σ)	Tau (u)	Eta (η)	W plus, W minus, and Z zero
Xi (Ξ)	Electron neutrino (ν_e)	(and many more)	Graviton
Lambda (Λ)	Muon neutrino (ν_μ)		X-particles
(and many more)	Tau neutrino (ν_τ)		

In the late 1970s a third lepton was found and dubbed the "tau" (τ). It is three thousand five hundred times more massive than the electron (a fat muon is the favored interpretation), but all tests show that it, too, has no internal structure and is pointlike. It also decays into many smaller particles.

You may be wondering how such massive particles can be considered pointlike and, therefore, by definition, elementary. Remember that mass is measured in energy units, the electron volt. To say that a particle has a great amount of mass is the same as saying that it contains an enormous amount of energy. A pointlike particle has no volume but it can have a great amount of energy.

Physicists don't know if any heavier leptons exist although many are sure that more will be found once more powerful machines are built. For now we have the three leptons (electron, muon, and tau) and their antiparticles, which have the same mass but the opposite electrical charge. Each of the three leptons also has an associated neutrino, and each of the lepton antiparticles has an antineutrino to keep it company.

Because neutrinos are neutrally charged, a neutrino and an antineutrino pair cannot have opposite charges like an electron-positron pair. Instead, they have opposite spins, that is, they spin in opposite directions. In the beta decay process that was discussed in Chapter Eight, it is actually an electron antineutrino that escapes unseen with the extra energy.

We designate a neutrino by the symbol: "ν." If it is an antineutrino, we put a line over it. This is done for all antiparticles. To distinguish the three different kinds of neutrinos, a subscript "e," "μ," or "τ" is used. Thus, $\bar{\nu}_e$ is the antineutrino involved in beta decay.

The listing and classification of all the leptons was relatively simple because there were so few of them. The same cannot be said for the hadrons, but that's another story.

12
"Three Quarks for Muster Mark"

THERE WERE TOO MANY HADRONS. Physicists realized by the late 1950s that some classification of those hundreds of newly discovered particles was necessary if any understanding of them was to be achieved. But where did one start? The distinction between baryons and mesons was helpful but it was not enough. However, each type of hadron could be identified by its many properties, such as spin and strangeness. Since some of these properties were shared with other hadrons, scientists found that it was possible to develop a classification scheme based upon these shared properties. You remember how Mendeleev in the nineteenth century constructed the periodic table by grouping the elements into families according to their characteristics? A similar method was now applied to the hadrons.

In 1961 two men, Murray Gell-Mann at the California Institute of Technology and Yuval Ne'eman, an Israeli physicist, independently developed a similar scheme. It became known as the "eightfold way," after the teachings of Buddha, because at first it predicted that all hadrons could be grouped into families of eight. Although physicists later found some families with more or less than eight members, the name remained. In fact, today we know that some hadron families may have one, ten, or even twenty-seven members. The eightfold way proved to be a marvelous theory. All known

115

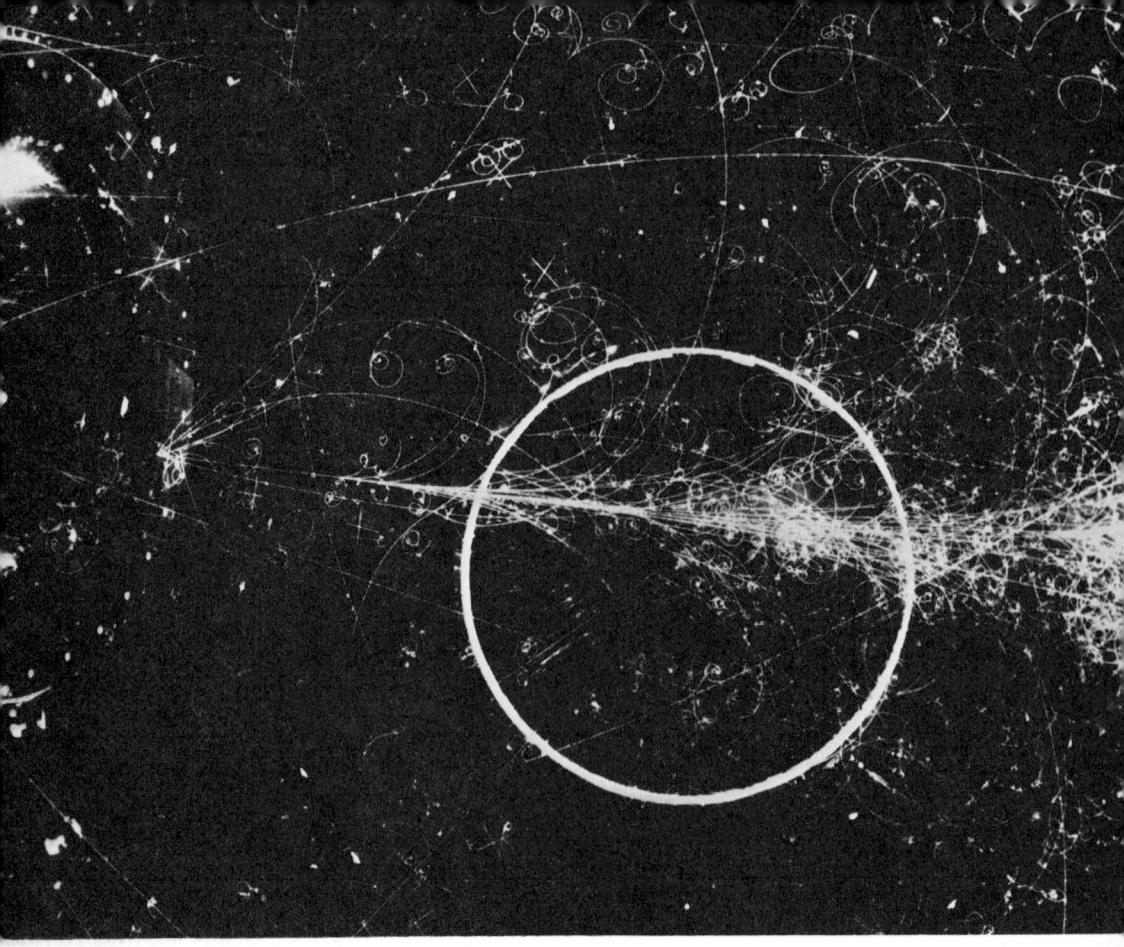

Fermilab.

Photograph of a particle interaction, taken in the fifteen-foot bubble chamber at Fermilab.

hadrons fit into it, each in its own family. The proton and neutron, for example, are members of a family of eight. The other members of that family are the lambda, the three sigma, and the two xi particles.

In 1962 Gell-Mann used the theory to predict the existence of an undiscovered particle, which he called "omega minus" (Ω^-). He said it would be the tenth member of a ten-member family. The following year, a group of experimental physicists at Brookhaven National Laboratory on Long Island,

New York, studied over fifty thousand bubble chamber photographs in an all-out effort to detect Gell-Mann's predicted particle. By November they had found it, giving further proof of the theory's validity. The elated scientists used the photograph of the trail left by the omega minus as that season's greeting card.

However, as when the table of periodic elements was first presented, no one knew why Gell-Mann's theory was so successful. What made all the hadrons fit so neatly into specific families? At that time hadrons were believed to have no internal structure or parts, and many scientists believed they were elementary particles. When they were smashed into each other in accelerators, all that came out were more hadrons, some of which were created from the energy of the collision. Yet, if hadrons were elementary, why was there a seemingly unlimited number of them? Why were some so massive? More powerful machines would supposedly produce only more massive hadrons, but none seemed capable of peering inside one.

It was time once again for theorists to come up with new ideas, new concepts that could be tested. Once again two scientists working independently of each other developed similar hypotheses. They were Murray Gell-Mann again and George Zweig, then in Geneva, Switzerland, although it was Gell-Mann's terminology that was adopted.

This new theory, which was presented in 1964, drew a parallel between hadrons and molecules. All the matter around us is made up of molecules. Each molecule is a collection of two or more atoms. There is an unlimited number of possible molecules but there are only a little over one hundred different kinds of atoms. In the same way, said Gell-Mann and Zweig, there is an unlimited number of hadrons,

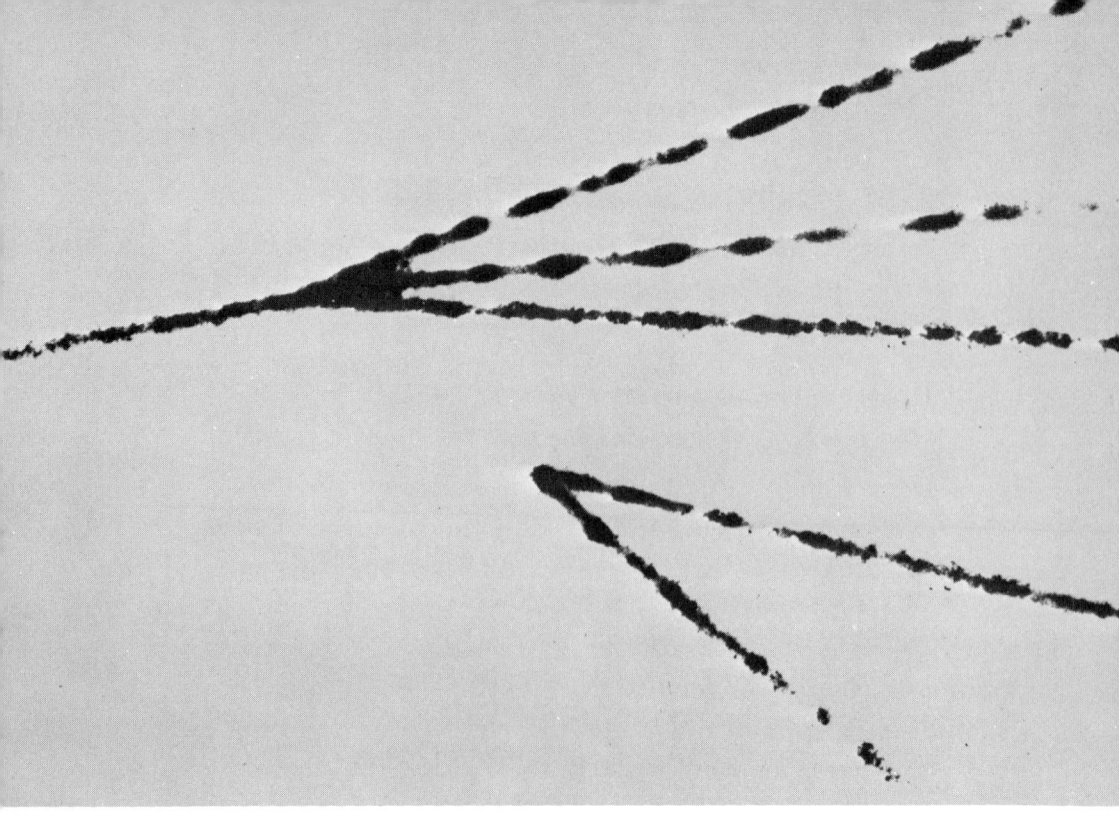

Stanford Linear Accelerator Center.

This photograph, magnified twenty times, shows the two particles created from the collision of a high-energy photon with a proton. Each particle carried a charmed quark. One of the pair (top) was positively charged and decayed into three conventional particles. The other was neutral and decayed into two charged particles. The distance the charmed particles traveled before decaying gave information on their lifetime.

but they are all made up of a very small number of more fundamental particles. Gell-Mann called these particles "quarks," from a line in James Joyce's novel *Finnegan's Wake:* "Three quarks for Muster Mark." "Quark" is a German name for a kind of cheese. Once again a whimsical name was given to a serious research object.

According to Gell-Mann's quark theory, quarks are point-like particles like the electron. And, like the electron, they also have a spin value of $\frac{1}{2}$. However, instead of having a whole unit of electrical charge, they have only fractional charges, and unlike the electron, they have never been seen as independent particles outside of a hadron.

Besides their electrical charge and spin, quarks have a very special property called "flavor." At first, some physicists even used the names of ice-cream flavors for the different quark flavors. These were never adopted but when describing a quark we still refer to its "flavor."

When Gell-Mann originally named these tiny particles, he thought that, like the three quarks mentioned in Joyce's book, there were only three flavors, or kinds, of quarks. They were called "up," "down," and "strange." The up and down names come from an early method of listing them and have no significance today. The strange quark is the one responsible for what physicists had been calling the "strange" property, or S-charge.

As with other quantum particles, each type of quark has an antiquark with the opposite electrical charge. Thus, the up quark has an electrical charge of $+\frac{2}{3}$; the anti-up quark's charge is $-\frac{2}{3}$. The down quark and strange quark both have charges of $-\frac{1}{3}$; their antiquarks have charges of $+\frac{1}{3}$.

Usually quarks are identified by just the first letter of their flavor, such as "u," "d," and "s." As with all antiparticles, a line over the letter denotes an antiquark of that flavor. For example, "$\bar{u}$" is an anti-up quark.

Baryons, which are those hadrons with half-integer spin values, are combinations of three quarks. Mesons, on the other hand, have only two quarks, which are always a quark and an antiquark. In either case, the quarks that make up any hadron must have electrical charges that add up to a whole number (zero being a whole number) because no hadron has a fractional charge.

Using the three original quark flavors presented in Gell-Mann's theory, physicists found that they could determine the makeup of any known hadron and explain its membership in a particular family. A proton, for example, is made up of two up quarks and a down quark (uud). A neutron is one up and two down quarks (udd). If you add up the electrical charges, you will find that in both cases the result is what is observed for these particles: $\frac{2}{3} + \frac{2}{3} - \frac{1}{3} = 1$ for the proton; $\frac{2}{3} - \frac{1}{3} - \frac{1}{3} = 0$ for the neutron.

The other six members of the proton-neutron family also have three quarks each. But in each case one or two of the up or down quarks of the proton or neutron are replaced with a strange (s) quark. Thus diagrams, such as Figure 19, which

Figure 19. AN OCTET OF BARYONS: THE PROTON-NEUTRON FAMILY

The letters in parentheses indicate which quarks that particle is made up of. Isospin charge (sometimes called isotopic spin) is another property that distinguishes each hadron. It is not the ordinary spin property that separates baryons from mesons.

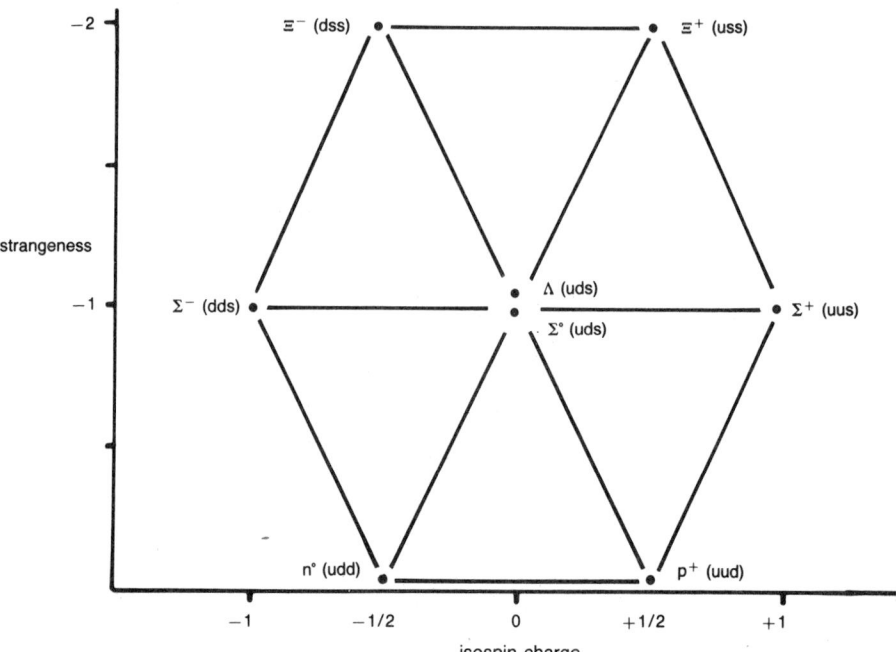

The letters in parentheses indicate the quarks of which that particle is made.

Figure 20. LEVELS OF MATTER

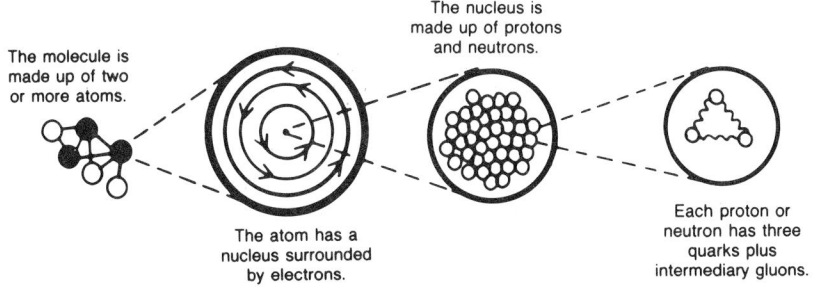

The molecule is made up of two or more atoms.

The nucleus is made up of protons and neutrons.

The atom has a nucleus surrounded by electrons.

Each proton or neutron has three quarks plus intermediary gluons.

show where each particle fits in, can be made for each family of hadrons. This is true for baryon or meson families. Such a diagram also incorporates another property, called "isospin charge," or "isotopic spin," which further distinguishes one hadron from another. Diagrams like these were developed after the introduction of the quark theory and explained why the eightfold way worked, much like the introduction of electrons, protons, and neutrons showed why Mendeleev's table worked.

As with atoms and molecules, there are many different ways in which quarks can arrange themselves within hadrons. This explains why the number of possible hadrons is very large if not unlimited. The quarks are thought to be orbiting each other within the hadron, moving constantly. There are many orbits that each quark can have. Each orbit corresponds to a different energy level and each combination of quark orbits makes a different hadron. Physicists usually only study the lowest energy configurations because these are the easiest to observe in the laboratories. The higher energy hadrons decay rapidly into those with lower energy and lower mass.

The quark theory revealed an entirely new level of matter. Like a series of nesting boxes (see Figure 20), each one smaller than the last, each new level has required a new technology to explore it. And as the bits of matter and the area to be probed became smaller, higher energies were needed to explore them. However, as you will learn in the next chapter, instead of detecting quarks with these greater sources of energy, the giant accelerators produced even more massive hadrons.

Most of these new hadrons could be readily identified and classified according to the quark theory. Although they were more massive than the protons and neutrons, they were no more unusual than any of the other particles that had been produced in earlier experiments. One of these hadrons, however, did not fit neatly into the classification system. It was found in 1974 by teams of physicists at two different accelerator laboratories.

At the Brookhaven National Laboratory where the omega minus particle had been detected in 1963, the Chinese-American physicist Samuel Ting and his colleagues were aiming a beam of protons at a metal target in an effort to create new matter. Their apparatus was designed to detect electron-positron pairs produced by the high energy collisions. Although such pairs are rarely created in these experiments, compared to the great number of hadrons that are produced, their appearance indicates the creation and decay of new kinds of matter, and studying them is very important.

For many months the Brookhaven experimenters set their detection devices to high-energy ranges. Then, in August 1974, after these ranges had produced no results, they tried several lower energy ranges. One, which was around 3.1 GeV, quickly proved to be what they were looking for. Many electron-positron pairs began appearing, each with a combined energy (or mass) of close to 3.1 GeV. And in each case

The electron-positron colliding beam storage ring, SPEAR, at the Stanford Linear Accelerator Center.

Fermilab.

the scientists found that before the sought-after pair was observed, a new short-lived particle was created. Although it rapidly decayed into the electron-positron pair, the particle lived long enough for its mass (in terms of electron volts) to be determined. Ting called this new particle a "J-particle."

At the same time, another group of scientists on the other side of the country, at the Stanford Linear Accelerator Center (SLAC) in California, was involved in a similar project. This team, headed by Burton Richter, used a ring called SPEAR, which is an electron-positron colliding beam storage ring, as described in Chapter Seven. In this ring, the colliding electron and positron annihilate each other but from their joint energy, other particles are created. The mass of these new particles depends upon how much energy is available.

By adjusting the energy of the original electrons and positrons, particles with specified masses are created more readily than any others.

Previous experimenters at SLAC had found that when the energy emitted by the collisions was around 3.1 GeV they got inconsistent results. Sometimes the detectors showed intense energy bursts but most of the time nothing happened. Bursts of energy indicated that new particles had been created, which was what the experimenters were looking for. Then, in November 1974, Richter and his team decided to make the energy range narrower than it had been before. Within hours they had zeroed in on the energy point they needed. At 3.105 GeV they received the strongest reading, indicating that they, too, had found the previously elusive particle. They didn't know about Ting's research and therefore called their particle a "psi" (ψ). When it was realized that both Ting's and Richter's particles were the same, the names were combined and the symbol "J/ψ" was adopted. Some now call it the "gypsy" (J/psi).

The gypsy didn't fit into the original quark model because it had certain properties that could not be attributed to the three known quarks. Instead, it was made up of a fourth quark flavor. This quark flavor had been suggested by theoretical physicists in the 1960s as a possible partner to the strange quark, but it could not be detected until higher energies were possible. It was called "charm" by physicist Sheldon Glashow because it "averted evil." In this case the averted evil was the possible failure of Glashow's theory, which will be described later. Charm represents another kind of charge, similar to the S-charge.

After the gypsy was discovered, other hadrons with charm quarks were found. Some were baryons and therefore contained three quarks. Others, like the gypsy, were mesons and had a charm-anticharm combination. As with other quark flavors, it is theoretically possible for a hadron to be made up of one, two, or three (baryons only) charm or anticharm quarks. The other quarks in the hadron can be any of the other flavors. However, all of the possible quark combinations within the hadrons have yet to be observed.

With the discovery of the charm quark, theorists predicted that once higher energies were available, more quark flavors with heavier masses would be discovered. Scientists were so sure of eventually finding these heavier quarks that even before they were detected, the fifth and sixth quark flavors were named "bottom" and "top." (Some scientists at first referred to them as "beauty" and "truth.") Then, in July 1977, Leon Lederman, now the director of Fermilab, announced the discovery of a very heavy particle, which he called the "upsilon." It was found to have a mass of 9.5 GeV and to be made up of a bottom quark and an antibottom quark. By 1978 more hadrons containing bottom quarks had been found and physicists were making jokes about "bare bottom" and "topless" hadrons.

However, in a more serious vein, with the discovery of the bottom quark, the top quark became the object of a massive search. The first evidence for it was found in 1983 by an international collaboration of a hundred fifty-one mostly European physicists working at the European Center for Nuclear Research (CERN) near Geneva, Switzerland. Bunches of protons and antiprotons were sent racing around CERN's accelerator ring in opposite directions at nearly the speed of light. By allowing them to pass through each other at certain points, occasionally a quark from a proton and an antiquark from an antiproton collided with and annihilated each other. This annihilation released the extremely large amount of energy needed to create heavier particles. Then it was necessary for the scientists to hunt through these millions or possibly billions of newly created particles to find the distinctive signature of hadrons containing top quarks. Six hadrons passed all the tests and more experiments in 1984 confirmed that the top quark had really been found. Heavier than even the bottom quark, the top quark has a mass of between 30–50 GeV.

Using the six flavors of quarks, each representing a "charge," physicists can now describe any hadron. (See Figure 21.) Each has a certain amount of each charge depending

Figure 21. QUARK CONTENTS OF SOME HADRONS

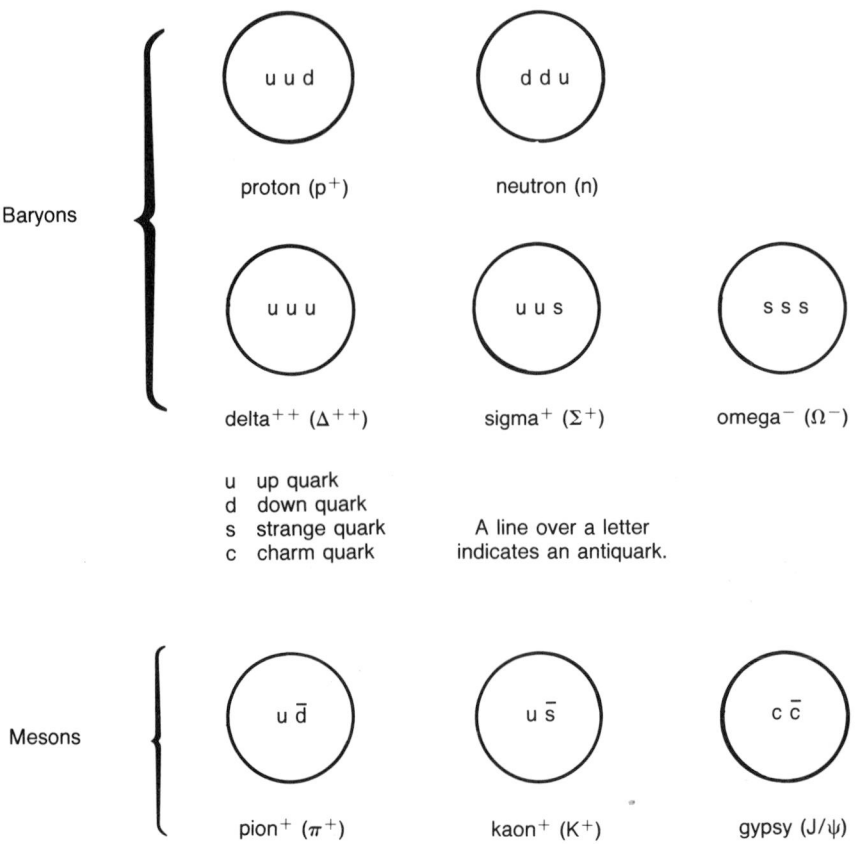

Table 5 GENERATIONS OF QUARKS AND LEPTONS

QUARKS		LEPTONS	
First Generation			
	electric charge		*electric charge*
Up (u)	+2/3	Electron (e⁻)	−1
Down (d)	−1/3	Electron neutrino (v_e)	0
Second Generation			
Charm (c)	+2/3	Muon (μ)	−1
Strange (s)	−1/3	Muon Neutrino (v_μ)	0
Third Generation			
Top (t)	+2/3	Tau (τ)	−1
Bottom (b)	−1/3	Tau neutrino (v_τ)	0

Note: For each particle, there is an antiparticle.

upon its quark makeup. The quarks themselves are believed to be elementary particles. They, along with the leptons and gauge bosons, are thought by many to constitute all the matter in the universe, the long-sought building blocks of nature.

To further classify these particles, recently physicists have grouped the quarks and leptons into what are called "generations" of elementary particles. As you can see in Table 5, the first generation consists of the up and down quarks, the electron, and the electron neutrino. These are the particles that make up all the matter in our everyday world. They are also the least massive elementary particles. As you already know, the electron is the lightest lepton and the up and down quarks are what make up the proton and neutron.

The second generation consists of the strange and charm quarks, the muon, and the muon neutrino. These particles are much more massive than those of the first generation, and those of the third generation are even heavier. That is why the hadrons containing top or bottom quarks need much more energy to come into existence.

Of course, there are also three generations of antiparticles. As with all other antiparticles, the antiquarks have electrical charges exactly opposite to the charges of their corresponding quarks.

Having found what most scientists now believe to be truly elementary matter, physicists still have many unanswered questions. Quarks have never been seen outside of a hadron. What force binds them so strongly, preventing their separation? How do the quarks and leptons interact with each other? These questions have been addressed by new theories but much of the proof will have to wait until larger, more powerful accelerators are constructed.

13

Universal Glue

WHEN THE QUARK THEORY was first proposed in 1964, many physicists regarded it with great skepticism, even though it did explain the differences between the many hadrons. But quarks, unlike electrons, cannot be seen, they said, so how do we know this mathematical invention describes reality? It wasn't until the late 1960s that experimental physicists had an answer to these skeptics.

At the Stanford Linear Accelerator Center (SLAC) physicists tried an experimental method similar to the one Rutherford had used much earlier in this century. A beam of electrons was sent crashing into a tank of liquid hydrogen at energies over 20 GeV. Because these high energy particles had very small wavelengths, the scientists believed that they should be able to use them to probe the interior of a hydrogen nucleus, which, as you know, is a proton.

Like the alpha particles in Rutherford's experiment, many of the high-velocity electrons went zipping right through the hydrogen without having their paths changed in any way. But quite a number did not have so smooth a journey. They hit something hard and their paths were noticeably altered. The scattered pattern of their paths showed that they had collided with some tiny particles within the protons. Nothing else would have had such an effect. These tiny particles were quarks. Here was the first direct evidence that protons were not elementary particles but, in fact, had an internal structure. Once again the results of an experiment were found to agree with theory.

Nevertheless, no quark has ever been seen; none has been isolated. They all remain hidden inside the hadrons. What is it that holds them so tightly within such a prison? By the early 1970s theoretical physicists had the answer in a new theory that suggested the presence of a superstrong interaction, one much greater than the strong nuclear one. This theory also described a new property of matter, called "color," that was somewhat like an electric charge. Particles such as quarks, the physicists proposed, possess the color property and therefore respond to this superstrong interaction, called the "strong color interaction." The term "color" distinguishes this force from the strong nuclear interaction that, you will remember, holds hadrons together in the atomic nucleus. Actually, as you will learn, these two strong forces are manifestations of the same phenomenon at different levels of matter.

Like "flavor," the term "color" has nothing to do with what we usually refer to as color. Quarks don't really come in different hues, but physicists did use the color names to distinguish the three different aspects of this property. They chose the primary colors of light: red, blue, and green. These colors produce white light when they are blended together. Antiquarks also have the color property, but their colors are the complements of the quark colors: anti-red, anti-blue, and anti-green.

Each flavor of quark and antiquark comes in each of their three respective colors. For example, there is a blue up quark, a red up quark, and a green up quark. There is an anti-blue anti-up quark, an anti-red anti-up quark, and an anti-green anti-up quark. In other words, according to this theory, there are actually eighteen kinds of quarks and eighteen antiquarks.

Although hadrons respond to the strong nuclear force, they are not as greatly influenced by the strong color force as are the quarks within them. According to the newly developed theory, this lack of response is because the hadron's "color charge" is neutral, or white. Like the real colors themselves, certain combinations of either quark or antiquark colors produce neutral tones. These combinations are the only ones possible when hadrons are formed. At any instant, for example, the three quarks in a proton will all be a different color: one red, one blue, and one green. It doesn't matter which one is the proton's down quark as long as the resulting color charge of the hadron is neutral. In the case of a meson that has only two quarks, this neutral color requirement is why one of the constituents must be a complementary antiquark. In that way the combination, such as green with anti-green or red with anti-red, always produces white.

In their theory, the theoretical physicists hypothesized that the strong color interaction, like the weak and electromagnetic interactions, also has mediating gauge bosons that are exchanged by the quarks, thereby holding them together within the hadron. These gauge bosons are called "gluons" because they are the glue that holds quarks together.

Like the photon, the gluon has no mass and its electric charge is zero. It moves at the speed of light, and as a boson, it has a whole-integer spin rate. The gluon spin is $+1$. However, unlike the photon and other gauge bosons, gluons possess the same property that they mediate—the color charge. They have color just like the quarks. But whereas each quark has only one color at any time, each of the eight types of gluons always possesses two color charges. These two colors do not have to be complementary as they do for the mesons. There can be, for example, a red-anti-green gluon.

Remember that the term "color" doesn't imply that these particles have an actual hue or tint. It is merely a way of distinguishing them according to their different properties. It might have been less confusing to have used other terminology, such as letters of the Greek alphabet, but this vocabulary is certainly more entertaining.

Because gluons have the color charge, they can interact between themselves as well as between quarks. This makes them quite different from other gauge bosons. The photon, for example, does not possess the electromagnetic charge that protons and electrons have and therefore cannot attract other photons or "stick" to other particles. It cannot absorb or emit another photon the way electrons do. But gluons attract each other and can stick to each other. They can also emit gluons and exchange them with nearby gluons. In fact it is possible that when enough gluons get together, they can form a composite particle, a sort of "glueball." This is one of the things that physicists are looking for in their research. As recently as 1983, it was suggested that a few had been detected in high-energy experiments.

But the gluons' main job is to mediate between quarks. Quarks constantly exchange gluons and in so doing, change their colors as well. For example, a red up quark may emit a red-anti-green gluon and thus be changed into a green up quark. (See Figure 22.) And the green down quark that might absorb this gluon will become a red down quark. As you can see, the flavor of the quark doesn't change in this exchange, only its color. The overall color of the hadron, too, stays the same neutral tone even though the colors of the individual quarks change.

Now, think back to the QED theory from Chapter Nine. That theory, you recall, gave a mathematical description of the photon's role in the electromagnetic force. To math-

Figure 22. GLUON EXCHANGE WITHIN A PROTON: AN EXAMPLE OF THE STRONG COLOR INTERACTION

The red up quark is converted into a green up quark when it emits a red-anti-green gluon. Red and anti-green charges are carried off by the gluon, leaving the green charge dominant. The gluon is absorbed by a green down quark, changing it into a red down quark. The anti-green of the gluon and the green of the quark neutralize each other, leaving the red charge dominant. Notice that the flavor of the quark is not affected by the gluon exchange, and the proton always remains color neutral.

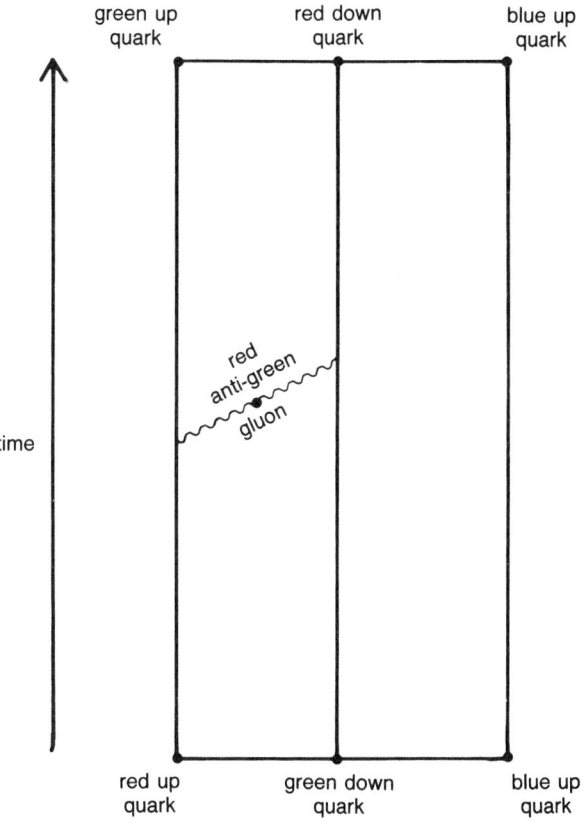

Proton with three quarks

ematically describe the role of the gluons in the strong color force, a similar theory was developed in the 1970s. It is called the "quantum chromodynamics theory" (QCD). Because there are three color charges and three anti-color charges, QCD is much more complicated than QED. These two theories, however, form the groundwork for many of the theories in quantum mechanics and particle physics that followed.

According to QCD, the exchange of gluons between quarks prevents them from breaking free of their hadron prisons. Other boson exchanges also keep particles together, but their effect diminishes as the distance between the particles increases. Just the opposite occurs with the strong color force: The gluons actually *increase* their control as the distance between the quarks gets bigger. This powerful control, one of the effects of the gluon's color charge, is called "quark confinement," and it explains why quarks have never been seen or isolated.

Physicists can mathematically define quark confinement but any attempt to describe it in ordinary language cannot represent a true picture because, as with other quantum phenomena, no one can really visualize it. However, several models have been put forth that give some idea about what is happening.

One, which is called the "bag model," pictures the hadrons as tiny bags in which even tinier particles, the quarks, are held. When two hadron bags are crashed into each other with great force in an attempt to break them open and free the quarks, the two bags combine into one at the moment of collision and jumble up their quarks. Then the combination bag breaks up into two or more bags, each a new hadron with its own quarks still confined as before.

Another model of quark confinement, called the "string model," pictures the quarks within a hadron as being attached to each other with strings. If the quarks are close to each other, the strings stay slack and the quarks can move

Figure 23. QUARK CONFINEMENT "BAG MODEL"

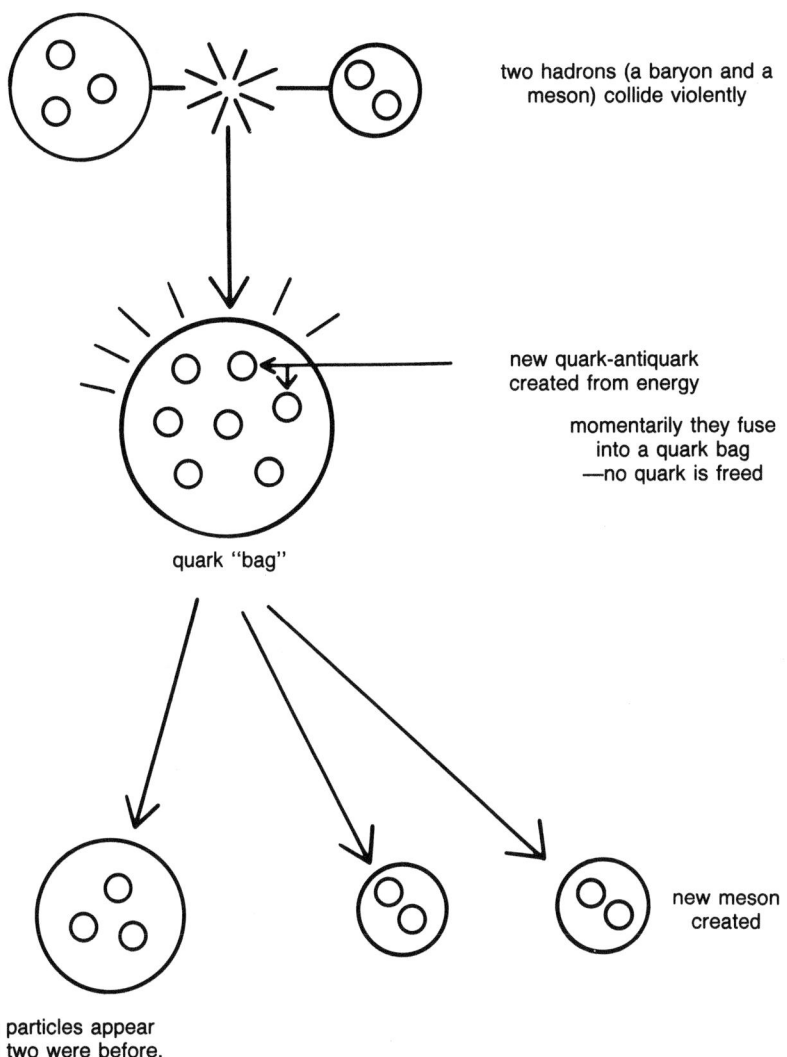

two hadrons (a baryon and a meson) collide violently

new quark-antiquark created from energy

momentarily they fuse into a quark bag —no quark is freed

quark "bag"

new meson created

three particles appear where two were before, but no quarks are seen

about freely. But if they are pulled away from each other, the strings become taut and the quarks' motion is more rigidly controlled. The greater the energy exerted in trying to break

Figure 24. QUARK CONFINEMENT "STRING MODEL"

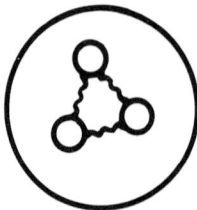

When quarks are close together as they are within a hadron, they can move about freely. The gluon "string" is loose.

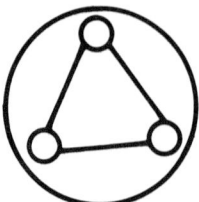

When they are farther apart, the string becomes taut, limiting their movements.

the strings and free the quarks, the more tightly the quarks are held.

Quarks are, therefore, forever imprisoned within the hadrons. Their release is only possible with energies much greater than physicists can probably ever produce on earth. Does this mean that quarks and leptons are the elementary particles that have been sought for so very long? Is this the end of the road? We don't know if more flavors or kinds of quarks exist. We don't know if more massive leptons will be found. Higher energies now being achieved in laboratories may very well create even more exotic hadrons with unknown and unpredicted quark flavors. But even if there are only six quark flavors and six leptons, many scientists feel that it is still too early to qualify these particles as truly "elementary." Remember that there are thirty-six known types of quarks and antiquarks, plus twelve leptons and antileptons, more in number than the known hadrons in 1950.

Because there are so many quarks, leptons, and bosons, and because more may be found as higher energies are reached, physicists have begun to look for other ways to describe the structure of matter. Instead of looking for yet a smaller level of matter, they are attempting to combine the many particles and interactions that are now known into one unifying theory. In this way, they hope to prove that there is really only one basic particle and one interaction and that all the differences we find around us are manifestations of an underlying unity. This search has taken physicists to other sciences, particularly the study of cosmology and astronomy, and has led them to explore the very beginnings of our universe when theoretically only one many-faceted particle and one interaction existed. It is there that they have found the "perfect symmetry."

14

The Search for Symmetry

THE LEFT SIDE of your body is almost the same as your right. On each side, for example, you have an arm, a leg, an eye, and an ear. We say that our two sides are symmetrical. But the symmetry is not perfect. You may have a freckle on your left cheek but not on your right one. One foot is probably a little bigger than the other. Most people are right-handed and do relatively little with their left hands. These are examples of "broken symmetries."

We can find many other examples of broken symmetries around us. The petals of most flowers are not arranged in perfect symmetry. A compass needle always points in one direction and not in any other. A door has its knob on one side and its hinges on the other. On the other hand, many wallpaper designs or snowflake patterns exhibit much greater amounts of symmetry. The drawing shown in Figure 25 is an example of a symmetrical shape.

Symmetry and broken symmetry are also found in the quantum world. In fact, physicists say the reason there are so many forces of such widely differing strengths and so many elementary particles is because of broken symmetry. To understand why they have come to this conclusion, we must go back some fifteen billion years, to the very beginning of the universe.

At that time our universe wasn't anything like it is today.

138

Figure 25 AN EXAMPLE OF SYMMETRY

Believe it or not, it was actually smaller than a proton. It was a tiny sphere filled with an extreme amount of energy. Its temperature was hotter than anything we can imagine. It had no atoms, molecules, or any other composite particles of matter in it. They could never have existed in such conditions.

Something, we are not sure what, triggered an enormous explosion of this energy and the tiny sphere began to expand very rapidly. This is how the Big Bang Cosmological Theory describes the creation of the universe. Although astronomers don't know what started the process, they have proved that this expansion is still taking place. And by measuring the rate of the expansion, they have been able to calculate how long it has been going on. This gives them the age of the universe —how long ago everything was still extremely compressed.

This calculation—fifteen billion years—is still a very rough estimate, however, because there are so many unknown variables involved. It may be as little as eight billion or as much as twenty billion years.

But we don't need to know the exact age of the universe to discuss its very early beginnings. Immediately after the Big Bang occurred, according to the latest theories of particle physics and cosmology, all the forces were unified into one single dominant force. The extremely high energy of the primordial universe allowed this condition to exist.

We cannot visualize this force any more than we can describe the exact conditions of the early universe. But scientists call it a complete or perfect symmetry. How can a perfect symmetry be described? It might be compared to the experience of swimming underwater in an extremely large pool, so large that you cannot see the sides or bottom. No matter where you look, everything appears the same. It is impossible to determine one direction from another. All appears equal.

A perfectly symmetrical place would also be extremely confusing to be in for any length of time. You would lose all orientation in space and time. There would be no landmarks for guidance. In a sense, time and space would cease to exist.

Of course, the primordial universe was not made of water. It was extremely hot and contained a tremendous amount of extremely compressed energy. The space that this energy occupied and the time that it took to do so were created by the Big Bang. Space and time did not exist before that momentous event, which marked the beginning of the universe.

It is very hard to imagine the primordial universe, and even physicists cannot readily describe it. Nor can they calculate, using their mathematical equations and theories, what the conditions were at the moment of creation and immediately afterward. There is a period of time that remains unexplored.

According to the Big Bang Cosmological Theory, once the Big Bang occurred, the universe expanded rapidly. As it grew, its energy density decreased. The photons' wavelengths, which had started out in the very short gamma ray region, became longer and longer. This original energy radiation continues to course throughout the still-cooling universe but at a much lower intensity than when first formed. Astronomers can detect it in the form of microwaves.

When hot steam cools off, it condenses into water. When the water cools enough, it freezes. Each of these changes is called a "phase transition." When physicists describe the cooling of the universe, they say it went through a series of "phase transitions" as it evolved into the universe we know today. This universe can be characterized as "frozen" even though it is still warm enough for us.

These phase transitions of the universe broke its perfect symmetry. Using the water in the giant pool as an example again, if the water cooled off and started to freeze, it would form into crystals of ice. It would no longer be the same freely flowing liquid it once was, and it wouldn't look quite the same in all directions.

In a sense, this is what happened to the young universe. As it cooled off, the interactions broke away from the symmetry one after another so that they no longer appeared the way they once did. Gravitation was the first to make its escape and exist as a distinguishable and separate interaction. This happened sometime before the first 10^{-43} second, the point beyond which physicists have yet been unable to go in their calculations or descriptions of the early universe. This moment, 10^{-43} second, is called "Planck time" after the German physicist who was a pioneer in the field of quantum mechanics and the first to recognize its importance.

Yes, 10^{-43} second is practically the very beginning of time, but so much happened during that first second that it is necessary to divide it into segments and examine each separately. At Planck time, the universe had a diameter of about 10^{-28} centimeter and a temperature around 10^{32} K. Remember that the diameter of an atom is only 10^{-8} centimeter, much bigger than the universe at Planck time. No accelerator today can approach the energies that existed then. Even the Tevatron is far short of the 10^{19} GeV needed to simulate conditions of Planck time.

The Big Bang created elementary particles out of this original energy, but because an enormous amount of energy was still present, the universe remained incredibly hot. At first, all of the newly created particles were able to change into one another by exchanging gauge bosons. As you will learn in the next chapter, some of these gauge bosons were to become extremely massive, whereas others, such as the photons and gluons, were to remain massless.

As the universe cooled and expanded further, other phase transitions took place. The energies decreased enough to stop the creation and exchange of the more massive bosons. Before the universe was one second old, the strong, weak, and electromagnetic interactions had broken from the original symmetry, and quarks and leptons were no longer able to be readily interchanged. In fact, quarks were already "frozen" into their hadron prisons, never to be seen again. However, no particles more complicated than a proton or a neutron had been created by then because the collisions of the existing particles were too violent to allow any to form. More complicated forms of matter had to wait until even cooler temperatures slowed down the particles, allowing them to coalesce.

Today we have the four seemingly different interactions, each with its own gauge bosons. We have the once free quarks now bound in hadrons, and we also have the relatively free leptons. These fundamental fermions all seem to be dissimilar, but most physicists are convinced that at higher energies these differences disappear. These very high energies cannot easily be reproduced but there are theories that attempt to describe these conditions mathematically.

What are these theories? They are called "unified field theories" because they refer to the interactions in terms of fields. You recall the electric and magnetic fields from Chapter Two. Maxwell's set of equations that combined electricity and magnetism into the electromagnetic interaction was an early example of a unified field theory.

The other interactions, the strong, weak, and gravitational, also involve fields in similar ways. Theoretical physicists seek to develop more advanced equations that will do for these interactions what Maxwell's equations did for electricity and magnetism. Their ultimate goal is a Grand Unified Theory, a GUT, which will prove that all four forces are really the same phenomenon appearing in different ways today because of the "freezing out" of the universe. The mathematical technique used to describe these fields is called a "gauge symmetry," hence these unification theories are sometimes referred to as "unified field gauge theories."

The first modern unified field theory to be proven successfully combined the electromagnetic and weak interactions. In terms of time since the Big Bang, these interactions were the last to break away or "freeze out" of the original perfect symmetry. Work on this theory began in the late 1950s but it was not until 1979 that the Nobel Prize for physics was awarded to Steven Weinberg, then of Harvard; Abdus Salam, a Pakistani physicist working in Trieste, Italy, and in London; and Sheldon Glashow from Harvard, for their achievement in theoretical particle physics.

These three men were the ones recognized by the Nobel Prize committee, but there were many others who participated in the theory's formulation. As you recall from Chapter Two, although Nobel Prizes and other awards are given to only a very few scientists each year, the projects and experiments honored are the work of teams of scientists, sometimes numbering in the hundreds. Without their cooperation with each other, many of the discoveries that have been discussed thus far would not have been made. The development of the unified field theories has also involved scientists from around the world, each contributing his or her expertise. The Glashow-Weinberg-Salam theory was the culmination of much of this work.

This theory's basic premise is that the electromagnetic and weak interactions are different aspects of the same thing. But how can that be? Their differences appear to be very great. For example, their strengths are not the same, nor is the distance at which their effects are felt. The particles that mediate the weak force, the intermediate vector bosons, have masses of about 80–100 GeV, whereas the photon has no mass at all. There are other differences between these two interactions but, according to the Glashow-Weinberg-Salam theory, all of them manifest themselves only in the ordinary world as we know it.

When the universe was 10^{-10} second old, its temperature was about ten quadrillion degrees. In any closed system, when the temperature goes up, particles move more quickly and collide with each other with a greater amount of energy. At ten quadrillion degrees, the primordial universe's energy reached 100 GeV or more, which was greater than the mass equivalence of the vector bosons, the W- and Z-particles. According to the Glashow-Weinberg-Salam theory, when the energy of the collisions (100 GeV+) exceeds the energy of the more massive particles (80–100 GeV), the symmetry of the forces is revealed. This symmetry, the theory continues, was lost once the energy of the universe fell below 100 GeV. Then, the individual forces "froze" into the way we see them today.

By combining the electromagnetic and weak interactions, the theory reduces the number of interactions to three— gravitation, strong, and "electroweak." The new force, the electroweak, represents a unification, which is a "hidden symmetry" in today's world. The four particles that mediate it are the photon, the W plus, the W minus, and the Z zero. It was the detection of first the W plus and W minus, and finally the Z zero particle in 1983 that provided the Glashow-Weinberg-Salam theory with direct experimental evidence.

The theorists' ultimate goal is to bring the strong and gravitational forces into this unification, but first they must attempt to combine the strong and electroweak. GUTs try to do this even though they do not involve the fourth interaction, gravitation. (See Table 6.) Modeled upon the QCD theory, GUTs also refer to the interactions in terms of fields, as did the earlier unified field theories, although reference to fields is usually omitted from their name. Proof of a GUT will be difficult because the energies required for any observational test are 10^{13} times greater than those needed to produce the W- and Z-particles.

Before we discuss the GUTs in greater detail, it is important to emphasize that in developing them, physicists worked backward in time. They found that first they had to unify the electromagnetic and weak interactions before they could consider the strong one. Ultimately they hope to be able to

Table 6 UNIFICATION OF THE INTERACTIONS

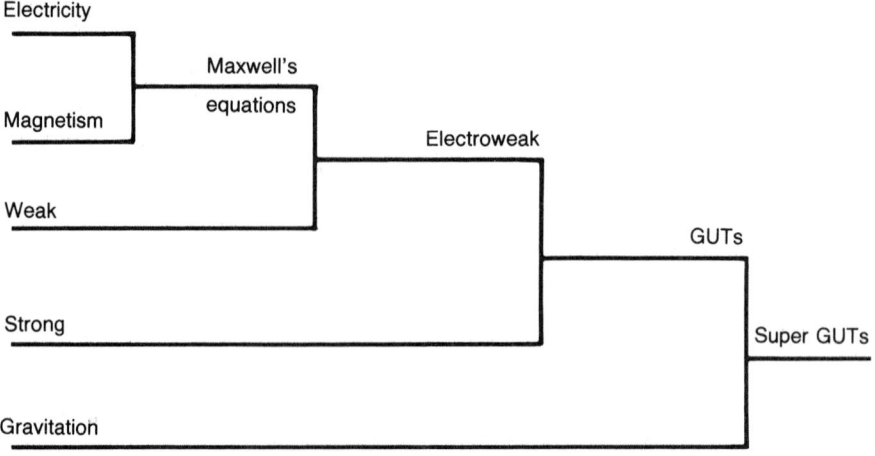

handle the gravitational force as well. By reversing this order, trying to unite the electromagnetic and gravitational interactions first, Albert Einstein was unsuccessful in his many attempts to develop a GUT. Physicists later discovered that this cannot be done without first considering the weak and strong interactions.

Many theories have been presented that attempt to unite the electroweak and strong interactions. New and sometimes very strange apparatus have been constructed for experiments that hopefully will either prove or disprove these new ideas. And as the results are learned, theories are revised and amplified—for a theory is only as good as the tests that support it. In the next chapter we will look at some of the tests that are considered to be most important in proving the validity of current theories.

15
The GUTs

ACCORDING TO A SIMPLE VERSION of Grand Unified Theories, after Planck time there were twenty-four massless gauge bosons. These mediating particles were responsible for the strong-electroweak interaction that existed at that time. With the further break of the symmetry, eight of these original bosons became the gluons responsible for the strong color interaction. Four others became the mediators of the electroweak interaction. The remaining twelve became "X-particles." X-particles possess a property that enables them to change a quark into a lepton or a lepton into a quark. According to this GUT, however, quark-lepton conversions are extremely rare. This is because when the universe cooled off and its symmetry broke, no more X-particles were created. Most of those then in existence decayed rapidly; and the few remaining acquired superheavy masses.

The W and Z bosons have masses of around 80–100 GeV but the X-particles' masses are calculated to be 10^{15} GeV, which is a quadrillion times the mass of a proton (about the mass of a human blood cell). Note, however, that although an X-particle may be as massive as a biological cell, it is structureless. Its mass is a measure of its energy content. This amount of mass is referred to as the "grand unification mass" and the corresponding energy is the "grand unification energy."

When collision energies rise above 10^{15} GeV, the differences between X-particles and gluons disappear and the underlying symmetry is seen. As you remember from the last chapter, the symmetry of the electromagnetic and weak forces is revealed at much lower energies.

By increasing the energy capabilities of accelerators, scientists have been able to find evidence of the more massive quarks and gauge bosons. They have also been able to show that unification of the weak and electromagnetic interactions does occur. However, no accelerator could ever create an X-particle today. Even under natural conditions their formation must be extremely rare because the particles require such enormous amounts of energy to come into existence. Scientists must therefore rely upon more indirect observational tests to verify or reject their hypotheses about X-particles.

According to the GUTs, X-particles have interactions that can destabilize protons and cause their decay. By means of an X-exchange, one of a proton's quarks is converted into a lepton. With only two quarks, the proton becomes unstable and decays. The detection of proton decay, therefore, is one way scientists hope to prove the existence of X-particles. (See Figure 26.) Because these particles are so massive, the probability of such an event occurring is very small, but it is not zero. Elaborate underground experiments with vast amounts of water are necessary because of the infrequency with which this process is believed to occur. Evidence of the decay of just one proton would give the X-particle theory an enormous boost in acceptance.

Another phenomenon predicted by the GUTs is "magnetic monopoles." These are very massive particles with an isolated magnetic pole. Theoretically, they were formed during that first hectic second after the Big Bang, and their number

Figure 26   FEYNMAN DIAGRAM SHOWING GUT PREDICTION OF PROTON DECAY

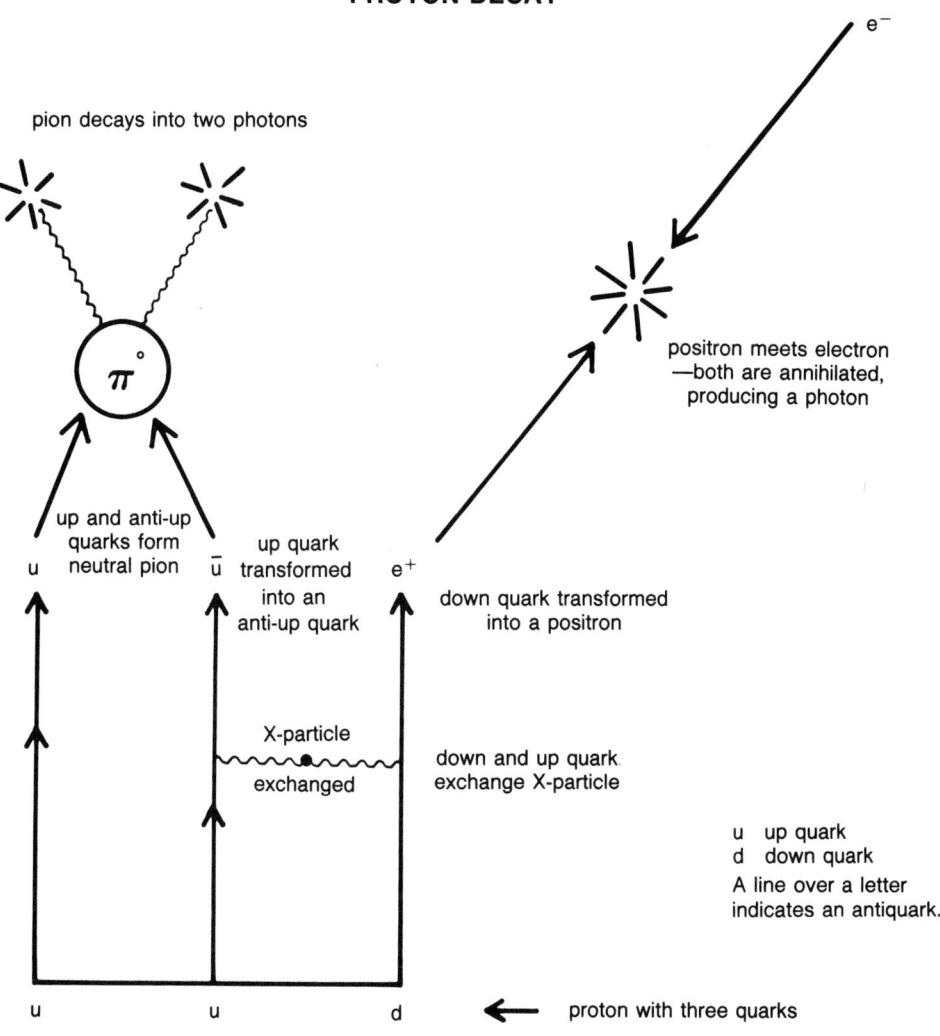

pion decays into two photons

$\pi°$

up and anti-up quarks form neutral pion

u

$\bar{u}$ up quark transformed into an anti-up quark

e^+

down quark transformed into a positron

e^-

positron meets electron —both are annihilated, producing a photon

X-particle exchanged

down and up quark exchange X-particle

u   up quark
d   down quark
A line over a letter indicates an antiquark.

u

u

d

← proton with three quarks

today, if they do exist, is very controversial.

The concept of magnetic monopoles is not a new one. They were hypothesized a century ago when experiments in electricity and magnetism indicated the similarity (and eventually the sameness) of these two forces. We know that an electrically charged particle can be either positive or negative. One can exist without the other. But any magnets we encounter always have two poles, a north one and a south one; they are always bipolar. Is it possible to have a particle with only one magnetic pole in the same way that an electron or proton has only one electrical charge?

According to the GUTs, the answer is "yes." At least that is how we would describe such particles, if they exist. Formed 10^{-35} second after the Big Bang, when the phase transition freezing the strong force occurred, monopoles are actually defects, or dividing points, caused by the uneven freezing.

When a lake freezes over during the winter, its entire surface does not become ice all at once. Small sections of it freeze first and then become enlarged until they meet other frozen areas. If you walk on the ice after the lake is solidly frozen, you can sometimes tell where these dividing lines occurred.

According to some GUTs, this is what happened to the young universe. Defects, or dividing lines, developed between regions where the symmetry froze out in different ways. They took three different forms: domain walls, strings, and points. "Domain walls" are two-dimensional defects that separate different regions of space. You might envision them as very thin sheets of gossamer material moving through a pool of water. A "string" defect is similar to the domain wall but has only one dimension instead of two. It is like a line drawn on a piece of paper. A "point" defect has no dimensions but is only a single dot in space.

These defects, according to theory, are very massive. Point defects, for example, may be as much as 10^{17} GeV. That's about the size of an amoeba, which is enormous compared to the particles we have been talking about. Besides this great mass, point defects also carry an isolated magnetic charge. We would detect them as magnetic monopoles. The other kinds of defects, the domain walls and lines, would be even more massive and may never be detectable. Physicists are not even sure what they should look for if they wish to find them.

In February 1982 no one knew how many monopoles existed in the universe and many doubted that any could ever be detected. For this reason, what happened on that Valentine's Day was a surprise to all. Blas Cabrera, a physicist at Stanford University, had set up an experiment based upon the premise that a moving monopole is a magnetic current just as a moving electron is an electric current. The moving monopole should therefore produce an electric field in the space around it. And if it passed through a loop of electrically conducting material, it should cause an electric current to flow in that loop. In this way any passing monopole would register its presence by a sudden increase of electrical current.

Cabrera used niobium wire for his loop and immersed it in extremely cold liquid helium. At such a low temperature, the wire becomes a superconductor; it has no electrical resistance. Any current sent through the loop would keep circling through it for months or even years.

No one was in the laboratory in which the experiment had been set up when the event occurred. Something went through the loop and caused the current to jump. Although no one actually saw what happened, many other alternative explanations have been ruled out. However, the phenomenon has not recurred so it cannot be studied further. Meanwhile, Cabrera has refined his apparatus so that it can detect a monopole coming in from many different directions. Thus far, however, no new ones have been detected by this better design. The longer it takes to detect more monopoles, if a monopole is what went through the original apparatus, the rarer they must be.

Meanwhile, the physicists conducting the proton decay detector experiment in the deep mine in Ohio have modified their apparatus so that it will signal the passage of a monopole through the pool of water as well as a proton decay event. They are watching for monopoles because a recently proposed theory suggested that monopoles may actually be responsible for promoting the decay of protons and neutrons. If this is so, proton decay experiments are certainly the largest monopole traps on earth.

Proton decay and monopoles are just some of the possible phenomena predicted by the GUTs. These theories have been able to provide rationales for many of the known phenomena that have puzzled the world of particle physics. Therefore, physicists would like to find direct substantiating evidence for them. The GUT theory discussed here is actually a very simple and early model. The final version is yet to be written.

However, even before the strong-electroweak unification GUT is proven, some physicists have started working on a GUT that will include gravity in the total picture. This would be a "supersymmetry" theory, a super GUT. Among other things, it would prove that bosons and fermions are manifestations of the same particle and can be transformed into each other in a fundamental way, just as the quarks and leptons are believed to be interchangeable by the actions of the X-particles. In other words, according to this super GUT, there is only one basic class of particles in the universe, and one force or interaction. This is how simple the universe supposedly was for the first 10^{-43} second. This simplicity is what the scientists are searching for.

It has been a long journey from Democritus's atom to the

super GUTs. Physicists describe the simplicity that they are searching for as the beauty that is inherent in the natural laws of the universe. Such laws do not change; they are universal and timeless. We can know of them only through observation and experimentation. Theory and experiment must go hand in hand along with the precision that mathematics brings to science. The quantum world of elementary particles is very bizarre and is not at all in concert with our preconceived notions about it. But research, theory, and experimentation have shown that these radical ideas are more correct than the older ones that they replace.

Gradually, as more and more people learn about these new discoveries and how they are changing our lives, our concepts about our universe will also change. Just as people several hundred years ago had to adjust to an earth that revolved around the sun (and not the sun around the earth), so we may learn to accept such concepts as the uncertainty principle and wave-particle duality. Without that acceptance, it is difficult for scientific thought to progress.

Appendix

THE GREEK ALPHABET

A	α	Alpha	N	ν	Nu
B	β	Beta	Ξ	ξ	Xi or Si
Γ	γ	Gamma	O	o	Omicron
Δ	δ	Delta	Π	π	Pi
E	δ	Epsilon	P	ρ	Rho
Z	ζ	Zeta	Σ	σ ς	Sigma
H	η	Eta	T	τ	Tau
Θ	θ	Theta	Y	υ	Upsilon
I	ι	Iota	Φ	φ	Phi
K	κ	Kappa	X	χ	Chi
Λ	λ	Lambda	Ψ	ψ	Psi
M	μ	Mu	Ω	ω	Omega

THE ELEMENTARY PARTICLES

QUARKS		LEPTONS	GAUGE BOSONS
UP	RED	ELECTRON	PHOTON
	BLUE	ELECTRON NEUTRINO	W PLUS, W
	GREEN		MINUS, AND
DOWN	RED	MUON	Z ZERO
	BLUE	MUON NEUTRINO	
	GREEN		GLUONS
STRANGE	RED	TAU	GRAVITON
	BLUE	TAU NEUTRINO	X-PARTICLES
	GREEN		
CHARM	RED		
	BLUE		
	GREEN		
TOP	RED		
	BLUE		
	GREEN		
BOTTOM	RED		
	BLUE		
	GREEN		

EACH PARTICLE HAS AN ANTIPARTICLE

THE ELEMENTS
Arranged according to their year of discovery

Elements Known in Ancient Times

NAME	SYMBOL	ATOMIC NUMBER	ATOMIC WEIGHT
Tin	Sn	50	118.69
Sulfur	S	16	32.064
Silver	Ag	47	107.87
Mercury	Hg	80	200.59
Lead	Pb	82	207.19
Iron	Fe	26	55.847
Gold	Au	79	196.967
Copper	Cu	29	63.54
Carbon	C	6	12.011
Antimony	Sb	51	121.75

Elements Discovered in Historical Times

NAME	SYMBOL	ATOMIC NUMBER	ATOMIC WEIGHT	YEAR DISCOVERED
Zinc	Zn	30	65.37	before 1400
Arsenic	As	33	74.922	1649
Phosphorus	P	15	30.974	1669
Platinum	Pt	78	195.09	c. 1735
Bismuth	Bi	83	208.98	c. 1739
Cobalt	Co	27	58.933	1742
Nickel	Ni	28	58.71	1751
Magnesium	Mg	12	24.312	1755
Hydrogen	H	1	1.008	1766
Fluorine	F	9	18.998	1771
Oxygen	O	8	15.999	1772
Nitrogen	N	7	14.007	1772
Manganese	Mn	25	54.938	1774
Chlorine	Cl	17	35.453	1774
Molydenum	Mo	42	95.94	1782

NAME	SYMBOL	ATOMIC NUMBER	ATOMIC WEIGHT	YEAR DISCOVERED
Tungsten	W	74	183.85	1783
Strontium	Sr	38	87.62	1787
Zirconium	Zr	40	91.22	1789
Uranium	U	92	238.03	1789
Titanium	Ti	22	47.90	1791
Yttrium	Y	39	88.905	1794
Chromium	Cr	24	51.996	1797
Beryllium	Be	4	9.012	1797
Tellurium	Te	52	127.60	1798
Niobium	Nb	41	92.906	1801
Tantalum	Ta	73	180.948	1802
Rhodium	Rh	45	102.905	1803
Palladium	Pd	46	106.4	1803
Cerium	Ce	58	140.12	1803
Osmium	Os	76	190.2	1804
Iridium	Ir	77	192.1	1804
Sodium	Na	11	22.99	1807
Potassium	K	19	39.102	1807
Calcium	Ca	20	40.08	1808
Boron	B	5	10.811	1808
Barium	Ba	56	137.34	1808
Iodine	I	53	126.904	1811
Lithium	Li	3	6.939	1817
Cadmium	Cd	48	112.40	1817
Selenium	Se	34	78.96	1818
Silicon	Si	14	28.086	1823
Aluminum	Al	13	26.982	1825
Bromine	Br	35	79.909	1826
Thorium	Th	90	232.038	1828
Vanadium	V	23	50.942	1830
Lanthanum	La	57	138.91	1839
Terbium	Tb	65	158.924	1843
Erbium	Er	68	167.26	1843

NAME	SYMBOL	ATOMIC NUMBER	ATOMIC WEIGHT	YEAR DISCOVERED
Ruthenium	Ru	44	101.07	1844
Cesium	Cs	55	132.905	1860
Thallium	Tl	81	204.37	1861
Rubidium	Rb	37	85.47	1861
Indium	In	49	114.82	1863
Gallium	Ga	31	69.72	1875
Holmium	Ho	67	164.930	1878
Thulium	Tm	69	168.934	1879
Scandium	Sc	21	44.956	1879
Samarium	Sm	62	150.35	1879
Gadolinium	Gd	64	157.25	1880
Praseodymium	Pr	59	140.907	1885
Neodymium	Nd	60	144.24	1885
Germanium	Ge	32	72.59	1886
Dysprosium	Dy	66	162.50	1886
Argon	Ar	18	39.948	1894
Helium	He	2	4.003	1895
Xenon	Xe	54	131.30	1898
Radium	Ra	88	226.05	1898
Polonium	Po	84	210.	1898
Neon	Ne	10	20.183	1898
Krypton	Kr	36	83.80	1898
Actinium	Ac	89	227.	1899
Radon	Rn	86	222.	1900
Europium	Eu	63	151.96	1901
Ytterbium	Yb	70	173.04	1907
Lutetium	Lu	71	174.97	1907
Protactinium	Pa	91	231.	1917
Hafnium	Hf	72	178.49	1923
Rhenium	Re	75	186.2	1925
Technetium	Tc	43	98.91	1937
Francium	Fr	87	223.	1939
Plutonium	Pu	94	242.	1940

NAME	SYMBOL	ATOMIC NUMBER	ATOMIC WEIGHT	YEAR DISCOVERED
Neptunium	Np	93	237.	1940
Astatine	At	85	210.	1940
Curium	Cm	96	244.	1944
Americium	Am	95	243.	1944
Promethium	Pm	61	145.	1947
Berkelium	Bk	97	245.	1949
Californium	Cf	98	246.	1950
Mendelevium	Md	101	256.	1955
Fermium	Fm	100	255.	1955
Einsteinium	Es	99	253.	1955
Nobelium	No	102	255.	1958
Lawrencium	Lr	103	257.	1961
Rutherfordium	Rf	104	261.	1964
Hahnium	Ha	105	262.	1967

SCIENTIFIC NOTATION

When using very large or very small numbers, scientists and mathematicians use "scientific notation." This avoids the necessity of having to write out a long string of zeros, and is easier to interpret quickly. This notation is used throughout this book and in practically all scientific texts.

You will find large numbers written in the following manner: 3×10^5; 1.5×10^8; 1.67×10^{-24}. To put these numbers into "nonscientific terms," we follow a very simple rule. The superscript number at the upper right of the 10 is called its "exponent." It indicates the number of places the decimal point must be moved in order to read the full value of the number. For positive exponents, we move the decimal point to the right; for negative exponents, to the left. Thus, 3×10^5 is the same as: 300,000.00 or "three hundred thousand." In the same way, 1.5×10^8 is: 150,000,000.00 or "one hundred fifty million."

$$1.67 \times 10^{-24} = 0.000\ 000\ 000\ 000\ 000\ 000\ 000\ 001\ 67.$$

We could also write it:

$$\frac{1.67}{1,000,000,000,000,000,000,000,000}$$

However, since it has far more zeros than we normally have words for (i.e., billion, trillion, quadrillion, etc.) we find it easier to say, "one-point-six-seven times ten to the negative twenty-four."

If the 10 with its exponent is given alone, it is assumed to be multiplied by 1.0 so that the above rule of moving the decimal point can be followed.

Note that although the exponents may differ by only a few numbers, this difference may represent a factor of many thousands. For example, 3×10^2 and 3×10^5 are 300 and 300,000, a difference of 299,700.

Glossary

Many of the words below have several meanings depending upon the context in which they are used. The definitions given here refer to the context of the study of particle physics and quantum mechanics.

ACCELERATOR: a machine that increases the velocity of charged particles, thus imparting great energies to them.

ALCHEMIST: a person who practiced alchemy, the art of trying to change base metals into gold or silver.

ALKALI: an element belonging to a specific group of elements, all of which possess similar properties, one of which is the ability to neutralize acids.

ALPHA RAYS: streams of rapidly moving helium nuclei (alpha particles); one kind of radiation emitted by the nuclei of radioactive atoms.

ANNIHILATION: the process that occurs when a particle and an antiparticle meet and their masses are converted into energy in the form of gamma rays.

ANODE: the positive pole of a battery.

ANTIMATTER: a form of matter that consists of antiparticles whose mass is the same as normal particles but with opposite electrical charges.

ANTIPARTICLE: for every subatomic particle there is an antiparticle of equal mass but opposite electric charge; for neutral particles such as the neutron and neutrino, the antiparticle has some other opposite property to distinguish it.

ATOM: the smallest portion of an element.

ATOMIC NUMBER: the number of protons in the nucleus of an atom of a given element.

ATOMIC WEIGHT: the relative weight of an atom of a specific element compared to atoms of other elements.

BARYONS: hadrons such as protons and neutrons that have half-integer spin values and are composed of three quarks.

BETA RAYS: streams of very rapidly moving electrons (beta particles); one kind of radiation emitted by the nuclei of radioactive
atoms.

BIG BANG COSMOLOGICAL THEORY: a theory that states that the universe started with an enormous explosion of primordial matter and energy.

BOSONS: particles, such as the photon and mesons, that have
whole-integer spin values.

BOTTOM: one of the six quark flavors; a third generation quark.

BUBBLE CHAMBER: an apparatus that makes the trails of subatomic
particles visible as rows of bubbles in a liquid.

CATHODE: the negative pole of a battery.

CHANNEL RAYS: the name originally given to a radiation discovered
streaming across cathode ray tubes in the opposite direction
to cathode rays; later found to be streams of protons.

CHARM: one of the six quark flavors; a second generation quark.

CHEMISTRY: the science of the composition of substances and their
effects upon each other.

CLOUD CHAMBER: an apparatus that makes the trails of subatomic
particles visible as rows of droplets that condense from a
supersaturated vapor or cloud.

COLOR: a property of quarks and gluons that is analogous to electrical charge.

COMPOUND: a substance composed of two or more elements that
are chemically united in specific proportions.

COSMIC RAYS: high-energy charged particles, most of which are
protons, which enter the earth's atmosphere from outer space.

COSMOLOGY: the study of the nature, origin, and history of the
universe.

CYCLOTRON: a circular accelerator that can raise the energies of
charged particles to several million eV or greater.

DECAY: the transformation of subatomic particles into more stable
particles; also the transformation of radioactive elements into
other elements.

DELTA: a particle created by the interaction between a proton and
a pion.

DENSITY: the mass of a substance per unit volume; for example,
how many atoms an object has per cubic centimeter.

DOMAIN WALLS: theoretical two-dimensional defects in the structure of the universe caused by early phase transitions as the
universe cooled off.

DOWN: one of the six quark flavors; a first generation quark.

EIGHTFOLD WAY: the classification of hadrons into families according to their properties.

ELECTRICITY: all phenomena caused by an electric charge, which is a property of certain particles.

ELECTROMAGNETIC FIELD: the region in which an electrically charged or magnetized body exerts its influence.

ELECTROMAGNETIC INTERACTION: one of the four interactions between particles; it is mediated by the photon and only charged particles respond to it; it is responsible for holding atoms together and causing them to interact with each other.

ELECTROMAGNETIC RADIATION: waves of energy associated with electric and magnetic fields that result from continual fluctuations in both fields, which are at right angles to each other.

ELECTROMAGNETIC SPECTRUM: the range of electromagnetic waves from the very short gamma rays to the longest radio waves. Visible light waves are found in about the middle of the spectrum.

ELECTROMAGNETIC WAVE: an energy wave whose energy depends upon its length and frequency; the shortest waves have the highest frequencies and the greatest energies.

ELECTRON: an elementary particle that is negatively charged. It is one of the three major particles found in a normal atom and was the first elementary particle to be discovered.

ELECTRON SHELL: any one of the many bands that electrons may occupy in an atom. Only a certain number of electrons may be in any one shell at a given moment.

ELECTRON VOLT (eV): a unit of energy.

ELECTRON-POSITRON COLLIDING BEAM STORAGE RING: an accelerator designed to send electrons and positrons in opposite directions and then crash them into each other to create new particles.

ELECTROWEAK: interaction that is a combination of the electromagnetic and weak interactions.

ELEMENT: a substance consisting entirely of atoms of the same atomic number; a substance that can be combined with other elements to form compounds but that cannot be broken down into any simpler substance once it is separated out of a compound.

ELEMENTARY PARTICLES: fundamental particles, the basic units of which all matter is composed.

ENERGY: the capacity for doing work, for exerting a force upon an object.

FERMION: any particle with a half-integer spin value such as the electron, proton, and neutron.

FEYNMAN DIAGRAMS: diagrams which symbolize complicated mathematical expressions of various interactions between particles in a simplified form.

FIELD: a region of space within which some force, such as magnetism or electricity, is felt.

FLAVOR: a name for certain properties of quarks and the particles they make up.

FREEZING: the change of the state of a substance such as from a liquid to a solid.

FREQUENCY: the rate at which the crest of any sort of wave passes a given point.

GAMMA RAYS: electromagnetic radiation with similar but shorter wavelengths than X-rays; one kind of radiation emitted by the nuclei of radioactive atoms.

GAUGE BOSONS: particles with integer spin values whose exchanges generate the interactions between other particles.

GAUGE THEORIES: a class of theories concerning the weak, electromagnetic and strong interactions.

GENERATIONS OF PARTICLES: the classification of all quarks and leptons into three groups or generations; ordinary matter is made up of first generation particles.

GLUONS: massless particles whose exchange generates the strong color interaction between quarks.

GRAND UNIFIED ENERGY: the energy at which the strong, weak, and electromagnetic interactions are unified (or identical); 10^{15} GeV.

GRAND UNIFIED MASS: same as Grand Unified Energy.

GRAND UNIFIED THEORY (GUT): a theory that describes the strong, weak, and electromagnetic interactions as the same phenomenon in different guises.

GRAVITATIONAL INTERACTION: the attraction of massive bodies toward each other caused by the exchange of gravitons between the bodies.

GRAVITON: a hypothetical particle whose exchange generates the gravitational interaction between massive objects.

GYPSY (J/PSI): the first particle to be detected that possessed a charm quark.

HADRON: any particle that participates in the strong interaction.

HIDDEN SYMMETRY: the symmetry between the interactions that is not apparent today because the universe is no longer as hot as it once was.

HYPOTHESIS: a supposition presented as an explanation of observed facts.

INTERACTION: a force between interacting particles that controls the behavior of those particles; specific exchange particles mediate each interaction.

INTERMEDIATE VECTOR BOSONS: see "vector bosons"; both names are used for the W- and Z-particles.

ISOSPIN CHARGE: (sometimes called isotopic spin) a property of hadrons expressed as a mathematical quantity; it is related to the spin and electric charges of hadrons in a particle family.

J-PARTICLE: the first particle containing a charm quark detected by Brookhaven physicists; same particle as the psi, causing its name to become J/psi or gypsy.

KAON: a K-meson, a type of strange meson.

LAMBDA: a particle that is one of the proton-neutron family; the first strange particle discovered.

LEPTONS: elementary particles with half-integer spin values that participate in the weak and electromagnetic interactions but not in the strong interaction.

LINEAR ACCELERATOR: a long, straight device used to accelerate particles to higher energies.

MAGNETIC MONOPOLE: a hypothetical unit of magnetic charge analogous to electric charge: normally magnetic poles are found in pairs, not singly as would be the case with a magnetic monopole.

MAGNETIC POLE: one of two points at which a magnet appears to have its magnetism concentrated; there is a north-seeking or positive pole and a south-seeking or negative pole.

MAGNETISM: the property of being magnetic or the force to which this is due; the branch of physics concerned with magnets and magnetic fields.

MASS: the amount of matter in an object.

MATTER: a form of energy; what all material things are made of; whatever occupies space and is perceptible to the senses in some way.

MESON: a hadron with an integer spin value composed of a quark and an antiquark; examples are pions and kaons.

MICROSECOND: one-millionth of a second.

MOLECULE: the smallest portion of a substance that can exist independently and retain the chemical properties of the original substance.

MOMENTUM: the product of an object's mass times its velocity.

MU-MESON (MUON): an elementary particle, one of the leptons, with a mass more than two hundred times that of the electron.

NANOSECOND: one-billionth of a second.

NEGATIVE POLE: the south-seeking pole of a magnet.

NEUTRINO: an elementary particle, a lepton, that is massless and electrically neutral.

NEUTRON: an electrically neutral particle, a baryon, that is a constituent of all atomic nuclei except that of hydrogen; a nucleon.

NUCLEON: a constituent of an atomic nucleus, i.e., a proton or a neutron.

NUCLEON RESONANCE: see "resonance."

NUCLEUS: the positively charged core of an atom; consists of one or more protons and, except for the hydrogen atom, two or more neutrons.

PARTICLE: a piece of matter that is smaller than an atom.

PARTICLE PHYSICS: the study of subatomic particles.

PERIODIC TABLE OF THE ELEMENTS: an arrangement of the chemical elements in order of their atomic numbers in such a way as to demonstrate the regular recurrences of certain properties.

PHASE TRANSITION: the change of a system from one configuration to another, usually with a change in symmetry as well; examples are melting and boiling.

PHOTOELECTRIC EFFECT: the emission of electrons from a substance when it is struck by a high-energy beam of light, usually ultraviolet.

PHOTON: an elementary particle whose exchange generates the electromagnetic interaction between charged particles; a quantum of electromagnetic radiation.

PHYSICS: the study of the properties of matter and energy.

PI-MESON (PION): the massive particle—about two hundred seventy times as massive as the electron—whose exchange generates the strong nuclear interactions between hadrons.

PLANCK TIME: 10^{-43} second after the Big Bang; the point before which theoretical physicists cannot yet calculate what conditions existed in the universe.

POINT DEFECT: a hypothetical particle created by phase transitions of the early universe that, along with string defects and domain walls, divides regions where symmetry is different.

POSITIVE POLE: the north-seeking pole of a magnet.

POSITRON: the positively charged antiparticle of the electron.

PROTON: a positively charged baryon found in all nuclei of normal atoms; a nucleon.

PSI: the first particle containing a charm quark detected by physicists at Stanford University; same particle as the J-particle, causing its name to become J/psi or gypsy.

QUANTUM (plural: quanta): one unit of energy; a photon is one quantum of electromagnetic radiation.

QUANTUM CHROMODYNAMICS (QCD): the theory of the strong interaction based upon the color properties of quarks and gluons.

QUANTUM ELECTRODYNAMICS (QED): the theory of the electromagnetic interaction.

QUANTUM MECHANICS: the system of mechanics that interprets physical phenomena occurring at the subatomic level of matter; evolved from the quantum theory and replaced classical mechanics in the study of particle physics.

QUANTUM THEORY: the theory which developed from Planck's description of energy as consisting of discrete units, or quanta, rather than a continuous flow.

QUARK CONFINEMENT: the control that gluons exert over quarks; the quantum phenonemon that explains why no quark has ever been isolated or detected outside of a hadron.

QUARKS: elementary particles which are one of the fundamental constituents of all matter.

RADIOACTIVE: possessing radioactivity; a property of spontaneous disintegration (decay) exhibited by certain unstable types of atomic nuclei.

RESONANCE: an unstable particle created very briefly by the interaction between a hadron and a pion.

REST MASS: the energy equivalent of a particle's mass while it is stationary relative to the observer.

SIGMA: a hadron; there are three kinds of sigmas: positive, negative, and neutrally charged; each has a mass of about 1,190 MeV; all belong to the proton-neutron family of particles.

SPIN: a fundamental property of subatomic particles describing the state of rotation of the particle.

STRANGE: one of the six quark flavors; a second generation quark.

STRANGENESS: the property of relatively slow decay exhibited by certain hadrons that possess strange quarks.

STRING DEFECT: a hypothetical one-dimensional object created by phase transitions occurring during the first second after the Big Bang that divides regions where the symmetry is different.

STRONG INTERACTION: the strongest of the four interactions, responsible for holding protons and neutrons together in the atomic nucleus and quarks together in the hadrons.

SUPER GUT: a theory that attempts to unify all the particles and interactions into one underlying class of particles that respond to one basic interaction; this would represent a perfect symmetry.

SYMMETRY: the corresponding sameness of parts of a figure on either side of any plane, line, or point; a circle is symmetrical on either side of any diameter that may be drawn through it.

SYNCHROTRON: a type of cyclotron that enables velocities close to the speed of light to be reached.

TAU: a lepton, identical to the electron and muon except for its large mass.

TEVATRON: the accelerator at Fermilab that includes the second ring of magnets within the main ring; capable of accelerating particles to 1 TeV.

THEORY: a formulation of apparent relationships of certain observed phenomena that has been verified to some degree.

THEORY OF RELATIVITY: a theory formulated by Albert Einstein that, among other things, presented the formula for mass-energy equivalence, namely: $E = mc^2$.

TOP: one of the six quark flavors; a third generation quark.

TRANSMUTATION OF AN ELEMENT: the changing of one chemical element into another.

TUNNELING: the process by which quantum particles can go through barriers that should be impenetrable according to classical mechanics.

ULTRAVIOLET LIGHT: electromagnetic radiation with wavelengths shorter than those of visible light.

UNCERTAINTY PRINCIPLE: a basic principle of quantum mechanics that states that for any instant in time the momentum and position of a particle cannot both be measured with complete accuracy; this uncertainty also applies to the energy of a system and time required to measure that energy.

UNIFICATION: the theoretical combining of two or more interactions into one set of mathematical equations, showing that the interactions are manifestations of the same phenomenon.

UP: one of the six quark flavors; a first generation quark.

UPSILON: the first particle detected that possessed the bottom quark.

VECTOR BOSONS: also called "intermediate vector bosons"; massive particles (W^+, W^-, $Z°$) whose exchanges generate the weak interaction.

VIRTUAL PARTICLE: a particle that is not in a "real" state although its properties can be calculated and its effects on "real" particles measured; exchange of virtual particles is responsible for the interactions between real particles.

VISCOSITY: the property of a fluid that affects its rate of flow.

WAVELENGTH: the distance between wave crests in any kind of wave.

WEAK INTERACTION: one of the four interactions; responsible for the decay of particles.

W-PARTICLES: two of the three kinds of vector bosons whose exchange generates the weak interaction.

X-PARTICLE: a very massive gauge boson predicted by GUTs as being responsible for proton decay by changing quarks into leptons and vice versa.

X-RAYS: electromagnetic radiation with very short wavelengths carrying high-energy photons.

XI: a hadron; there are two xi particles, each with a mass of 1,320 MeV; both are members of the proton-neutron family of particles.

Z-PARTICLE: one kind of vector boson whose exchange generates the weak interaction.

Index

italics indicate illustration